A BRITISH SUBJECT

A BRITISH SUBJECT

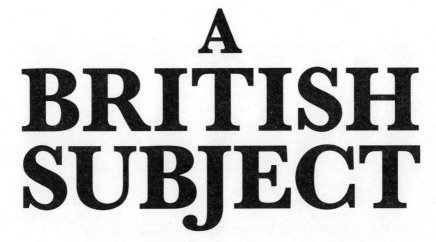

*How to Make It as an Immigrant
in the Best Country in the World*

DOLAR POPAT

Foreword by David Cameron

Biteback Publishing

First published in Great Britain in 2019 by
Biteback Publishing Ltd
Westminster Tower
3 Albert Embankment
London SE1 7SP
Copyright © Dolar Popat 2019

ISBN 978-1-78590-525-4

10 9 8 7 6 5 4 3 2 1

A CIP catalogue record for this book is available from the British Library.

Set in Baskerville

Printed and bound in Great Britain by
CPI Group (UK) Ltd, Croydon CR0 4YY

This book is dedicated to my guru, Morari Bapu, whose teachings have been guiding me for thirty years, and my wonderful family, who have brought me so much love and joy.

CONTENTS

FOREWORD BY DAVID CAMERON

The story of the Ugandan Asians is like something from a novel. Driven from their homes, country after country turning them away, then Britain welcoming them in. Through determination, talent and a strong set of values, they became one of the most successful groups of immigrants anywhere in the history of the world.

This is the story of thousands of people who arrived with nothing, but put everything into making a fresh start. I don't think it has been brought to life with more warmth, compassion or vividness than it has here, in the memoirs of my friend Dolar Popat.

I first met Dolar when I was the leader of the Conservative Party in opposition and he was a Conservative activist. At that time, our party was facing a conundrum. Voters from black and ethnic minorities often shared our values and outlook, but they didn't tend to vote for us.

A large part of my modernisation plan for the party was to make it more open to people from all backgrounds. Dolar was a driving force in that endeavour: organising, corralling, chasing, dictating and offering wise counsel, from nurturing candidates of Indian origin to launching the Conservative Friends of India. Working alongside him, I saw a man who was guided by family, faith, political conviction and a deep love of his country. As he puts it so beautifully in this book: 'The UK is my second god.'

Our work paid off. In the 2015 election, 49 per cent of British Indians voted Conservative – a huge increase on the 11 per cent we received in 2005. In 2005 there were just two Conservative MPs from ethnic minorities; by 2015 there were seventeen. The Conservatives were, for the first time, the most popular party among Hindus and Sikhs.

Of course, Dolar's expertise goes beyond politics. He is a businessman and a pioneer in small-business finance. After 2008's financial crash, when credit started to dry up, Dolar was the perfect fit as both a whip and a business minister. Then, as it became clearer that the UK needed to extend its horizons when it came to trade and investment, the role of trade envoy to Uganda and Rwanda had his name on it.

Reading this book, I felt sad learning of the abuse Dolar suffered as a schoolboy and the racism he faced here in Britain. These are things I didn't know about him. But what I do know about Dolar – his unique character – shines through in these chapters.

First, we get an insight into his work ethic. His many-plates-spinning, night-oil-burning determination to work and work until the job (or in his case, several jobs) is done to the absolute best of his ability.

The second thing that comes through is his humility. I have seen that self-effacement over the years, including when he simply didn't believe I was appointing him to the House of Lords. Dolar is one of the most modest people you could ever meet.

The third of Dolar's qualities that comes across is his uncompromising attitude towards what ought to be done to make things better. He is tough on many issues, from philanthropy to global trade to integration. He can say things that no one else in his position can – and in this book, he does.

This feels like the right book at the right time. One of the biggest questions for the world at this moment is how we can integrate new communities successfully. That question is even more urgent as we see more migrants on the move than at any time since the Second World War. We could do worse than refer to Dolar Popat's story. As a British, Hindu, Ugandan, Indian, Gujarati businessman and politician, he proves that multiple identities cannot only coexist, but can help people to flourish.

For years, people have urged Dolar to tell his story. He's always been too humble – and too busy. So I'm glad he took the time to stop, sit down and write about his life. It is as instructive as it is inspiring. It should be read by people who want to learn about the history of Africa, India and Britain. It should be read by immigrants who are newly arrived in Britain. It should be read by those who are keen to get ahead in politics and business. And it should be read by anyone who wants to know how our country has become such a global success story. I believe we are the greatest multi-racial, multi-religious democracy on Earth – and that is in large part down to Ugandan Asians like the author of this book. I hope you enjoy Dolar's story as much as I did.

David Cameron
June 2019

1

GETTING OUT

I didn't know the name of the British man in the beige safari suit. He was probably one of the colonial officials who had remained from the time of Empire, before Uganda became independent from Britain in 1962. Nine years later, everything and nothing had changed. A new President, Milton Obote, had come and gone, very recently ousted in a coup by Idi Amin. Politically, the country was in chaos. But there were still old Brits like this on the golf course, even now, in February, the hottest time of the year. African summer, but winter in my heart.

From the shadow of some bushes, I watched the man swing his club, making an arc through the air. There was a *tok* and I saw the white ball fly up in the direction of the Rock, the cryptic elevation that rises above Tororo to a height of nearly 1,500 metres. Tororo is the town in eastern Uganda where I lived with my parents, not far from the Kenyan border. I felt resentful as I watched the ball ascend. Its certain movement upwards somehow seemed to represent something I felt was impossible for me to achieve in my own life. For in those days we Asians were stuck – stuck between newly postcolonial Europeans and newly independent Africans, and fully accepted by neither. (Although at that time Asians and Africans did still share the fact we were both barred from being members of the golf club.)

There was more to it than that, though. Maybe in many ways I was just another depressed teenager (I was seventeen in February 1971). But I didn't know what depression was; in my world then, the word barely existed. If I saw a kid of that age acting as I was, and you asked me now, I'd say obviously this poor chap is depressed.

I had not gone back to high school when the spring term started, and felt I had no prospects. I had finished my O levels in December and failed all eight of them. Another reason for my low spirits was the fact that my best friend – my only real friend – Ignatius Coelho, was planning to leave the country.

A third reason for my depression was something that had happened the previous month, on 25 January 1971 – the day of Amin's coup. We were taking Kumud, my sister, to the airport at Entebbe; aged twenty-one, she was flying to England to continue her studies. Our car was full – my father, me, Kumud, my nephew Sanjay, my older sister Sumitra and her friend Ninette, all packed in. As we approached the terminal, something felt wrong. There were a lot of soldiers, and an air of anxiety. But we made it into the airport and waited for the flight. It was meant to leave at 10.30 p.m. but was delayed till midnight.

On the stroke of midnight, more soldiers came running in, about fourteen or fifteen of them. There was a Milton Obote picture in the concourse and the very first thing they did was take that down. They didn't smash it, like I heard happened at some other places, they just hid it – I think behind one of the ticket desks – as if they were not sure of themselves and feared Obote might return. Then they found the airport managers and told them to cancel all the flights.

Kumud's flight was duly cancelled, and at one in the morning we were ordered to vacate the airport.

So we got back in the car and made for Kampala, intending to stay with a cousin. That 21-mile journey from Entebbe to Kampala was the longest of my life. Tanks on the road. A lot more roadblocks than usual. The car radio told us of the coup. I will never forget the harrowing sight of bodies lying along the roads. We arrived at our cousin's house, very shaken.

The next morning we went out to get food at around 7 a.m. It was a mistake. There were more bodies, scattered everywhere, and all the shopfronts were smashed. No one was around; it was like a ghost town. We could hear the sound of gunfire in the distance. After being threatened with guns by soldiers who were much more aggressive (perhaps these men were more confident than those we'd encountered at the airport, who must have been among the coup's first movers), we scurried back to my cousin's house, shocked and upset.

At around 4 p.m. we plucked up the courage to head homewards. Across Kampala, the Ugandans were celebrating the overthrow of Milton Obote. Smiling and gesticulating in our vehicle, we pretended to join in the celebrations and thus managed to sneak out of the city.

Once we were underway, it was another journey of checkpoints, fear and harrowing sights. Blood was smeared across some of the soldiers' guns and shoes. After four gruelling hours we reached Tororo, where we were immediately met by a group of about thirty people asking us what had happened. The Ugandan newspapers didn't print on the day of the coup – probably uncertain of whether they should support Amin or not – and people were anxious for information. But at least we'd made it home safely.

In the month after the coup, Amin made lots of speeches pledging service to the nation and holding out the hand of friendship to Ugandans of every stripe. Even then, I knew it was nonsense. I had seen those bodies.

These were the thoughts playing on my teenage mind as I skulked on the edge of the golf course in Tororo. (There is a saying in the town: 'The Eiffel Tower is to Paris as the magnificent Tororo Rock is to Tororo district.' Or perhaps it should be the other way round – our lives in those days were a long way from Paris.)

I was born near Tororo in 1953, in a village called Busolwe, a very poor place where Africans scraped a mainly agricultural living. My father – along with a few other Asian shopkeepers – supplied the community with soap, tinned food and other basic commodities.

Named Amarshi Haridas Popat, my father was born in 1918. He left India for Uganda in 1938. After reaching his destination, he first secured a job and then began trading on his own account. Following several years working alone, he was joined by my mother, Parvatiben. Born in Porbandar (also the birthplace of Mahatma Gandhi) in 1920, she met my father in India and they married there. I never knew my grandparents on either side as they had all passed away by the time I was born, but I do know that my paternal grandfather was in the jute business in the Indian state of Gujarat during the 1890s.

There were a lot of us in our immediate family: three daughters (Sudha, Sumitra and Kumud) and five sons (Manoj, me, Pankaj, Suresh and our little brother Kantesh). The village was without electricity or running water, or any modern conveniences at all. Everybody knew everybody else's business. There were nine other Asian families living in Busolwe, and we tended to hang out with them. My mother relied on these families during a bad period in 1955 when my father had to return to India for medical treatment and she was left on her own. He was in fact critically ill, and she did not know whether he would return. Even though I was only two at the time, I remember that absence vividly. With our successful store we were probably doing the best among the local Asian families before my father left. But in his absence the store was robbed and we were soon poor. We effectively went from riches to rags.

I was incredibly fond of my father and really missed him during this absence; every time a car or bus came into the village I'd run to it eagerly, hoping he'd returned. It was a particularly difficult time for my mother. She was incredibly worried and we didn't get any news or updates; it didn't help her mood when I drank what I thought was a bottle of Coke that turned out to be paraffin. I was quite ill, but I recovered, and my father came back OK in the end.

My mother was very kind. She was a typical Gujarati house-wife, dedicating herself to her role of supporting and serving the family. She was forever cooking, cleaning and checking on the children, but she was sheltered from a lot of the world outside our house. She was naïve about our education and the money that came into our house. Although I always got on well with my mother, I was naturally more drawn to my father's entrepreneurial and more daring spirit.

I strongly believe that in order to continue progressing in life, it is essential to continue remembering your roots. My parents' values of thrift and hard work have had a huge influence on me and I wouldn't be where I am today without them. Some of my earliest memories are taking the bus to Tororo from Busolwe with my father and spending many happy hours as he bought stock for his shop, joining a gaggle of Asian shopkeepers at a succession of wholesalers. He liked to talk to me about who had bought what from whom.

In fact, I was enthralled by my father and his business. As a child I was quite hyper and for others possibly too much to handle, but my father was forever patient with me. Although he had a temper with others, I always seemed to escape it, even when I pushed him.

In October 1962, my father shifted the business from Busolwe into Tororo, a town twenty-two miles away.

We didn't live above the shop, moving in above another next to one of the town's main roundabouts. Although my father owned the freehold of the shop in Busolwe from which we were getting some rental income, it wasn't sufficient, and making the books balance was a real struggle. We were a big family and money was always tight. To put things into perspective for Western readers, we had enough to eat but not enough for all the children to have shoes; I was bought my first pair when I was eleven. So the atmosphere in the house was happy up to a point, but also pressured.

It was to this house on the roundabout I would return on that February day in 1971 after I had spied on the British man at the golf course, musing on whether my bad outcome so far as a human being could be improved on. I was in no hurry to get back home. A cloud of family shame hung over me.

My pensive return took me past the residence of my former headmaster at Rock View Primary School, Mr Grewal. He was not my favourite person and I was not his: I was always his target for some reason and received almost daily beatings from him. On one of these occasions, when I was twelve, the beating was particularly severe and humiliating. Grewal beat me very hard with a cane, reducing my buttocks to a mulch of flesh, in front of the whole school (280 people). He hit me so fiercely that his turban almost fell off.

In Tororo town, they used to have a fete; it was run by the Lions Club charity, of which Mr Grewal was a distinguished member. This particular year, the fete had a lucky dip stall. You gave a shilling and you picked a ticket, trying to get a number that matched one of the items on offer. There were forty or fifty things to try and win, ranging from boxes of candles to radios. But the main item of desire was a very nice, expensive-looking clock – number 21.

Ahead of time, I had bought my own book of raffle tickets (you know how all those books of coloured tickets look the same); when I was stood at the stall, I chose a number from my book that matched a good prize, hid it in my hand, then put my clenched hand into the bowl of tickets. I started by 'winning' something small, and then added four or five other things, too. Ingenious. Next I plucked up the courage and, what do you know, I got number 21 and won the clock!

I got found out, of course. What I hadn't known was that the people running the stall had purposefully left out number 21; the clock was just to lure the punters in. I was gaming a system that had already been rigged. Thus the beating from Grewal. Admittedly, I had deserved punishment, though not of such a violent kind. And because the caning was in assembly, the whole town knew about it. This incident stayed with me like a stain, from the age of twelve through my teens. I was completely outcast, like a criminal who has been in prison and just come out. There goes Popat the cheat, Popat the fraud – all the time. It was also degrading for my family.

It was partly the Lions Club. The Lions Club was an enormous force in these quasi-colonial societies at the time. It was just absolutely extraordinary the way its members controlled the whole show. I'm sure there was an element of money involved. I think if I'd been from a wealthy family, my punishment would have been much less severe. But being poor compounded my fate; it was as if I deserved double punishment because we didn't have a lot of money *and* I'd been caught.

So that was the beginning of my downfall, the effects of which crystallised in my mind that day on the edge of Tororo golf course. That beating by Grewal started all the problems in my life. It was followed by a series of other beatings from him and from other teachers, for even tiny misdemeanours. Sometimes they beat me about the head. But the worst was Grewal and my hands. I was left-handed and he saw writing with the left hand as nothing less than a crime. He used to hit me with a ruler on my left hand so I didn't use it. Those four years or so after the fete incident were the worst of my life; I was depressed, living under the shadow of the shame my scam had caused and fearful of physical injury.

At one point it all got so bad that a doctor took pictures of my wounds and bruises, but my father could do nothing about it. Combined with the hatred the other Asian students conveyed to me, these beatings had a long-term negative impact on my self-esteem. My father was probably the most understanding. 'They were there to rob you and you robbed them,' he would say of the lucky dip affair, but he was a lone voice. This sense of being a pariah continued on during my disastrous educational career at Manjasi High School (the high school I went to after Rock View, and from which I left with no O levels). The teachers there were good, mostly English expats, but I was too mentally damaged for them to help me much.

The effects of all this lasted a long time. I used to have nightmares every so often, even weeping in my sleep, my wife tells me, fearing someone was going to beat me. These bad dreams have thankfully subsided.

Apart from Ignatius Coelho – my best friend, and in the year above – I had no Asian friends at Manjasi. There were thirty Asians in the school, all day boys, and about 300 African boarders. In my class, the eight other Asian boys sat in pairs while I sat with the Ugandans, whom I loved by default, I suppose. I used to sit next to Bob Kimoimo, who later played football for Uganda's national team. After arriving in London, I wrote three letters to Bob over three years, but never heard back from him. In 2016, one of my old teachers, Roy Godber, who has now retired in Canada, heard about my success and came to see me in Parliament, along with two Ugandans. I mentioned Bob Kimoimo having been murdered by Idi Amin (which is what I assumed had happened) but, joy of joys, the Ugandans said he was still alive and working as an engineer at Entebbe Airport. They put me in touch with him and, during my next trip to Uganda, he came to see me at the Serena Hotel. We were both in tears and hugged having being reunited. To this day I am still in contact with him.

It truly makes me ashamed to look back at how Asians treated Africans in those long-ago days. Some African house boys were working seven days a week for poor pay, but instead of being treated with respect, they were constantly sworn at by their Asian employers. It was inhumane. There was no doubt we Ugandan Asians were racist for not mixing with Africans. There is much less of that today. On some level, however, I think the Ugandan Asians of the 1970s deserved the fate that eventually came to us. Not all of my fellow Ugandan Asians would agree with me, but there it is.

Anyway, at high school it was the Ugandans whom I hung out with, and who most supported me in the various money-making schemes that consumed most of my attention. These were partly a way of supplementing our family income and partly because an instinct for business was somehow just there in me, bubbling away in my Gujarati DNA. Maybe these schemes were also a form of displacement activity, directing my attention away from my educational failures and emotional distress.

My most cunning strategy was getting a local cinema to put on films, which I advertised to boys at school by saying there would be girls there from a neighbouring school (Tororo Girls School, where my sister Sumitra was a prefect). I then went to the girls and told them there would be boys at the event. I usually showed something a bit risqué as the sexual element worked well for the youngsters of such a conservative community. The 'Carry On' films were particularly popular, especially *Carry On Doctor*. To top it off, I bought biscuits and sweets wholesale and sold them at the showing. I made more money at these events than the cinema owner!

These cheeky childhood schemes were my first deals. Partly, that is what this book is about: the entrepreneurial spirit and how it creates business. Along with politics, this has been the matter of my life. I am not ashamed of making money. No one should be. However, as I have got older – and the significant influence of my guru, Morari Bapu (whom I and his followers lovingly call Bapu), is important here – I have learned that business shouldn't be just about the quick buck, but about finding a type of activity that is personally and socially sustaining: one which, as well as a profit, generates a margin of 'truth, love and compassion'. These are Bapu's watchwords, and in time they would become my own. I have learned that it is quite feasible to reconcile an entrepreneurial drive with one towards spirituality. As my friend Kamlesh Madhvani puts it: 'If one reads the *Gita* [a Hindu spiritual book] it reveals that the essence of Karma Yoga involves being able to fulfil one's duties to familial and societal wellbeing, but not being attached to the fruits of action.' It's good to make money, but don't fall in love with it.

In some ways, the seeds of my turning towards the more spiritual aspects of life were sown in Uganda when, not long after the tombola incident, I had the honour of encountering the Hindu religious leader, Yogiji Maharaj.

It was at the temple in Tororo, a warehouse-like building with low ceilings but good lighting due to around six floor-to-ceiling windows. Although it was not a typical place of worship – a few shops were integrated into the building, probably to provide some commercial income – it still captured the feel of a traditional temple. About 150 Hindus would attend each weekend.

Making his first trip from India to east Africa, Yogiji Maharaj was famous in our community and beyond, somebody people revered. The day I saw him he was wearing the familiar orange robes of a Hindu priest. He was about 5ft 10in., slim and had a sun-bleached face. Surrounded by people, Yogiji Maharaj was emitting holiness like a light, full of power and strength.

I saw all this through one of the large windows, as children were not allowed in. While I appreciated Yogiji Maharaj's special presence, I acted as though I didn't. In a rebellious mood, I was pulling faces, doing my best to irritate everybody. Someone came out and I expected another beating.

Instead, I got called inside by Yogiji Maharaj, who proceeded to bless me by tapping me on the shoulder. With this sign of acceptance, he gave me love when I really needed it, and won my heart.

This was my first real contact with a Hindu spiritual leader. At such an unhappy time in my life – I wasn't just unhappy in myself, I was unhappy with the whole human race, and I wanted to believe in something – it was like having a new best friend.

Beyond recounting first the dawning and then growth of my spiritual awareness, and telling the story of my life in its successive phases, my more explicit purpose in writing this book is to show how it really is possible to make it as an immigrant in Britain, however un-British your background apparently is and however poor your family background.

I say 'apparently is', because like many Ugandan Asians, my family were British Overseas Citizen (BOC) passport holders, which included a subset known as those with British protected passports. People's situations were slightly different depending on where they were in east Africa. Uganda was a British protectorate until independence, whereas Kenya was a British colony; so, Ugandan Asians got a British protected passport and Kenyans got a British subject passport. For a time, a Kenyan passport provided the right of abode in the UK, but this didn't apply to the Ugandan version. (Eventually, the legislative situation would change for *all* BOC passport holders.)

Either way, this official status turned out to be a very different thing from *being* British, despite the welcome that would be given to many Ugandan Asians by Britain. Being British takes time and effort, and genuine willingness on the part of the immigrant as well as the host nation. A Ugandan British protected passport offered you some rights to protection and passage but not – at least not in the first instance – any certainty that you could remain in Britain once you had arrived.

The role of Asians in east Africa is complex and has a long history, which I shall try to explain, focusing on the story of the region's Gujaratis, my own particular group. Suffice it to say for now, though, that there were enormous tensions between the Asians and Africans in Uganda, as well as many genuine bonds – commercial and institutional more than personal, but bonds all the same.

At first, despite the shock of the January 1971 coup, some Asians, especially those who were not Ugandan citizens, felt (like many in Uganda and abroad) that Amin might be a good thing for the country, sweeping away the economic reforms that Obote had put in place to address inequality (which broadly threatened Asian interests) and either relaxing regulation over citizenship applications or speeding up the enormous backlog for those 12,000 Asians whose applications had been left unprocessed for years. But my family were unpersuaded by Amin's fake magnanimity and conciliatory father-of-the-nation bullshit: we had seen the writing on the wall.

We were not being paranoid. With the advent of Idi Amin's rule, we knew our time was up in Uganda. It had become apparent, even with Obote moving towards socialism and Africanisation, that there would soon be no opportunity for BOC passport holders to apply for a licence to trade. This didn't affect full British citizens themselves, or at least not yet (and many of these expats were protected by a big company such as Chillington Tools or by a quasi-diplomatic institutional infrastructure, such as the Colonial Development Corporation). But in 1971, it was clear to us what our situation was as owners of a small family business. We had applied for Ugandan citizenship for the whole family but it was taking a long time to process, along with the 12,000 others.

We were not alone in rejecting the illusion of Amin being the nation's 'Big Dada', the jolly giant who would fix all of Uganda's problems. Having lost their licence to trade, many Asians were making plans to leave before they were pushed. However, the main exodus would not happen till the following year when, in early August 1972, Amin was to order the expulsion of thousands of individuals of South Asian descent in Uganda.

Way before this, however, there was a pervasive climate of Indophobia, in part a product of a tacit British policy of using the Asian population as a buffer between black and white. Within months of Amin coming to power, he would be threatening to take away the right to work of Asians who weren't Ugandan citizens, and issuing particular decrees to do with identity documents that applied solely to Ugandan Asians.

This picture, of an early postcolonial tension between inclusion and exclusion, was one that Amin would go on to exploit during the rest of 1971 and into 1972, but to an extent shades of this tension already existed within the complex communities of newly independent African countries, between tribes as well as ethnic incomers like us Asians.

This tension wasn't particular to Uganda, though it was most acute there. As Lord Steel noted:

The problem for the Asians in east Africa started not in Uganda but in Kenya, with the Africanisation programme of the Kenyatta Government. At that point, the Asian population of Kenya was less than 2 per cent of the whole. Sadly, in 1967–68, when they [Kenyan Asians] started to come to Britain because of the Africanisation programme, there was a great controversy in this country about what should be done about it – against the wishes of people like Iain Macleod and Hugh Fraser, who had been the Ministers responsible at the time of independence of these territories. They had given the Asian – in fact, the whole expatriate – population two years in which to opt either for local citizenship or to retain British citizenship. Many had retained British citizenship, but the government of the day decided to introduce the Commonwealth Immigrants Act 1968, which withdrew that fundamental right of entry into this country.[1]

My early experiences of being an outcast within my own group caused me to become aware at a young age of the need for openness and tolerance of others. Sitting with the Ugandans at school and not with my own kind opened my mind. The experience of public shame that led to this understanding was unfortunate, but it definitely created more love and affection in me for my fellow human beings, regardless of who they are, what colour they are or how disadvantaged they are.

These days I am known (among other things) for being a figure of standing in the Gujarati community in Britain, but this has always been on the basis of joining in with others – not just other minority groups, but also the British majority (indigenous but a very mixed bag, historically speaking). Collaboration is very important to me: not just the notion of integration, so often spoken of by politicians of both right and left, but its actualisation through deeds and actions,

---

1   Hansard, HL Deb, 6 December 2012, vol. 741, col. 808.

such as joint ventures between community groups. And it all really began because I sat with the Africans rather than the Asians at school.

When I got home from the golf course that night in February 1971, my mother was cooking a simple dish of rice and dal, and my father had his head down over his account books from the shop. I was very aware of the enormous financial burden he was carrying as a self-employed person with a large family, in a foreign land full of dangerous political uncertainty.

In days gone by, my elder brother, Manoj (who was eighteen months older than me), would have been pedalling away at a sewing machine. He used to do sewing jobs from all around Tororo district. Like the money I made (or some of it), his income had gone into a family kitty. But on that day I returned from the golf course, Manoj was already in England, having gone there in 1970 to try to get work.

We who were left in Uganda were still reeling from the near escape we had had on our way back from Entebbe, while trying to get my sister out. Kumud had, in fact, followed Manoj to England a few weeks after the coup, but now a big question mark hung over what would happen to the rest of the family.

That night, after we had eaten, I told my father that I too wanted to go to England. I had heard that my friend Ignatius was going, you see. Given he was a year ahead of me in school, I had missed him when I was in my final year at Manjasi. Really, he had been my protector, telling other boys to leave off when they teased me. He was a cool guy, Ignatius: tall and handsome, of Goan extraction, he wore his hair slicked back in those days and sported a leather jacket. He was like an Indian version of the Fonz from the American TV show *Happy Days*. Every girl in town fancied him, and we'd often take walks with them up the Rock, me playing the role of the gawky stooge, or go down to the river, where Ignatius's father worked as a municipal water engineer. I guess Ignatius taught me that if you were going to be branded a rogue, you might as well do it in style.

But this was not the most important thing about Ignatius. The real reason he made friends with me was because he had religious values. He was a serious Catholic, like many Goans. Perhaps he also felt something of an outsider too, as a Goan among Hindus who were then super-conscious of caste and other differences.

Our friendship seemed in jeopardy now that he was leaving, just as the idea of an Asian future in Uganda seemed in jeopardy, too.

My father had no problem with the idea of me going to England, and neither did my mother. We knew that our time was up in Uganda and my father's intentions were for all the family to go to the UK, and my leaving meant I would no longer be dependent on them in the meantime. Over the next fourteen months all of us still in Uganda would leave one by one.

Manoj and Kumud had gone on student visas and the plan was that I would do the same. This route out was obviously not open to my parents, but my father had already applied for a voucher scheme that the UK government had for BOC passport holders, allowing them to settle in Britain. Introduced by Harold Wilson in 1968, the intention of this special scheme was to prevent mass immigration into the UK from the Commonwealth, but at the same time the legislation did try to recognise the specific hardship being suffered at that time by BOC passport holders and their dependants – these were people under political pressure to leave their newly independent countries of residence, but who held no other citizenship and had nowhere else to go.

So – I could go to Britain if I wanted, knowing my parents would almost certainly follow. The problem was money. There was hardly enough for us to survive on day to day as a family, never mind buy any more plane tickets. But once parental permission was granted, I put my mind to earning enough, working every hour that God sent for a trading company called Khosla. Their main business was a supermarket predominantly for British customers: a specialist grocery for expats who at that time had not seen through Amin. He appeared to be Britain's man, you see, a Cold War proxy, tacitly approved by the Foreign Office and MI6 as someone one who would stop Obote's move to the left.

I just focused on keeping my job and collecting my pay packets. I would often think about that time later on in my life, while facing big challenges, commercial or otherwise. You just have to get on with it – eating the elephant in small bites, as the saying goes.

Within five months, I had amassed the 1,600 shillings I needed to buy a ticket. In early May, I went to the British High Commission in Kampala. I remember walking round outside, thinking, 'What should I do? How do I get in?' I was nervous, obviously. Luckily, when I entered the building, there was no queue, nothing. I handed in my application and my passport. They called me into a room and interviewed me for ten minutes. My spoken English was pretty good by Ugandan Asian standards; a lot of my peers spoke mainly either Gujarati or Swahili. Immediately, they gave me a student visa for six months.

On hearing of my intention to join him, Ignatius had delayed his own departure. Thus it was that on 24 May 1971 we travelled together to Entebbe Airport, taking the same route my family had taken with Kumud at the start of the year. I was full of '5 p.m. on a

Friday evening' excitement, like I was finally going to be free from all my emotional baggage.

My father came to the airport with us. His final words were something to the effect of, 'Work hard, get a job' – that kind of thing.

By the time we left Uganda, the military and political situation was much worse, as Amin had begun ramping up the anti-Asian rhetoric; the famous expulsion speech the following year (in fact given in Tororo, to troops of an airborne division) would culminate in the claim that 'Asians milked the cow but did not feed it'.

Even the usually cool Ignatius felt the fear on that journey to the airport, as we passed through two military checkpoints, weaving our way between nail-studded tyre traps. And then we had to get through Immigration and all that. It was nerve-racking; once we were in the plane, we were thinking, 'Oh, what a relief.'

I got on that plane less than a month before my eighteenth birthday. I brought with me £10 of my own money in my wallet, £200 of banker's draft in sterling that I was bringing over for someone else and a suitcase made of cardboard. The suitcase was packed with thin clothes made by Indian tailors on the streets of Tororo – totally unsuitable for the British climate, even in May. That was all I had. We were too nervous to bring much with us because of the searches at military checkpoints. People had far fewer possessions in those days, anyway – a lot of the stuff we have now is just clutter, to my mind.

Obviously it was very emotional to leave my parents for the first time and take my first flight, too. I remember thinking, 'Oh, Krishna, is this thing really going to go up into the air?'

It was a KLM flight, with a stopover in Amsterdam. I was so green that I was amazed by the announcement on the tannoy in the cabin. I thought they'd come and talk to each passenger individually!

My main fear was how to find a job and make ends meet. We were coming to a country of uncertainty, and the only things we knew about Britain were what we had been told, or what had been written on a blackboard when we were not paying due attention. The *Uganda Argus* and other Ugandan newspapers were filled either with local battles or stories focused more on the Eastern Bloc; it wasn't like we could research a country on the internet as you can now.

The only comfort was that I had my sister and my brother in Britain already. However, Manoj didn't even know which day I was coming – there was a postal strike on in Britain at the time – but he had at least had enough notice to organise a place at a college for me and Ignatius. Somehow we got a message to Ignatius's cousin José and it was agreed that he would meet us at Heathrow.

There were not many people on the plane and I felt lucky to have Ignatius with me. In the time since leaving Manjasi he'd been to study in India, but hadn't enjoyed it. He'd come back to Uganda and now, sat on that plane, was talking about whether he would like England. As I have said, Ignatius had long been my protector, but I think he also felt comfortable being with me.

He was genuinely going to England to study, and even said that he wanted to go back to Uganda afterwards and be a teacher. But me? I wanted to prove myself, to show I was not a write-off, which is how everyone but Ignatius thought of me. Part of that was certainly repairing my bad education, but that was not my only reason to come to Britain. Deep down, I think I wanted to exercise my entrepreneurship. It's something that resides in your core, like a concert pianist's talent; it lives in you and is sparked by the various situations in which you find yourself.

So that is what brought me to Britain, the formerly barefoot boy. I don't think I am unusual. The number one priority of most immigrants, after all, is to seek security – to work hard, make money, save money, buy your own house if possible. That is more of a priority for first-generation immigrants than, say, achieving a professional qualification. This is particularly true of Gujaratis, who would also nearly always prefer self-employment over employment. (But I don't think that feeling is exclusive to this group.) All this vigorous activity of immigrants adds to the wealth of the host country – but any policy on this subject has to be firm as well as fair.

During the flight, I sensed more anxiety in Ignatius than normal. We were both lost souls, I guess. We weren't Ugandan; we weren't Indian; and we may have had a British protected passport, but we weren't British yet. India's out, Uganda's out, so we were on our way to our third and probably final option.

But something happened on that plane: I suddenly began to feel free. An internal voice said, 'OK, Dolar, you're an adult now, driver of your own self.' It had begun talking even as we lifted off over the dusky silver expanse of Lake Victoria, which I could see from my window seat, and continued all the way to Amsterdam.

Sometime during that journey I had my first beer to celebrate becoming a man, one who has the opportunity to make a clean start. A man leaving behind him not just Idi Amin but those other people, too: the headmaster who tortured me; the fellow Asians who shunned me (some of whom I have since bumped into at Gujarati gatherings round the world). I'll show you, I thought, as I sipped my beer and began admiring the pretty, well-dressed Dutch air hostesses. They brought round food on little trays. This Western food with its profusion of meat was strange to me, as we were mainly vegetarian at home, but I ate it, thinking that I had better get used to it.

Schiphol Airport was a breeze, as it has continued to be ever since. I remember the security guard plucked someone's hat off his head and then put it on again. They both laughed and everyone in the queue laughed, too. It wouldn't happen now. During the stop-over, Ignatius and I wandered through the vast airport and saw escalators for the first time. Then we caught a smaller plane to London, which was completely full.

However, our first experience of England as we arrived at Heathrow was one of confusion. We were not sure what to do, so we followed the other passengers and read the signs to go through Immigration. But then we were detained for about four hours.

After a long wait, an official began bombarding us with questions: 'How long are you here for?'

'Is this a real college you're attending?'

'Have you come here to study?'

'How long are you really here for?'

'What do you intend to do in your studies?'

'What courses are you taking?'

Then we were separated and taken aside by other officials and asked the same questions all over again.

You must not think I am complaining. These border officials were doing their job correctly, even though they looked at me like I was already a convicted criminal. There was very strict immigration control in those days, like there is now, but officials were much less polite. East Africa was an area they looked at especially closely, because in 1968 a large number of Kenyans had come to Britain and settled, getting in the door before Harold Wilson's voucher bill went through.

The college Ignatius and I were going to was Woods Tutorial College on Hampstead Heath, and little did I know, but forged letters of admission to it had been circulating in east Africa.

Based on those forged letters, the British High Commissions in Uganda and Kenya had been handing out visas nine to the dozen, so the immigration officers wanted to make sure we were bona fide students.

My admission letter was genuine, as was Ignatius's. The immigration officers rang the husband-and-wife principals of the college at home and they confirmed this. But we learned that Woods was in fact not quite as we'd imagined.

2

GETTING ON

When we finally emerged from Immigration at Heathrow, Ignatius's cousin, José, was waiting in Arrivals. By then it was very late, nearly one o'clock in the morning as I recall. 'Why have you been so long?' he asked. We explained and he took us in a taxi to a rented house in Fulham – 316 Fulham Road. There were four girls there, all Irish and Scottish, and not enough beds. Ignatius and I slept on the floor, exhausted.

I suppose the priority that next morning should have been to find my brother Manoj, but Ignatius and I had other ideas: we went straight to Trafalgar Square! There was a Pitman's College there and Ignatius was trying to get admission for his girlfriend, Roma.

Typical Ignatius. The first thing he does on arriving in Britain is try to help someone else. Roma was still back in Tororo and wanted to join him.

Once we had made the enquiries, we went to see the lions round the fountain in Trafalgar Square, scattering pigeons as we larked about. You know, those lions were a powerful symbol of the British Empire to us colonials. There is a photo of me and Ignatius standing next to one of those great stone beasts, smiling happily. And we *were* happy; it was as if my bad memories of Uganda and Ignatius's bad memories of India were being already lifted away on the wings of the pigeons.

As for 'empire', which has become a negative word now, you have to remember that for us Ugandan Asians, it was then still representative of the idea of a mother country, a place where we might be nurtured as individuals (which certainly was not happening in Uganda or India), however much we understood the oppressive nature of colonialism.

Believe me, I am not being historically naïve when I write this, but stating a psychological fact. I think some of the stateless people who come to Britain as immigrants today think of the country in the same way (even those from outside the Commonwealth), which is why they want to come here rather than settle in other European nations. The attraction is not just British opportunities, it's also a question of the British ethos.

Even though my father was Indian, the connection we felt was with Britain. Something intangible made it so appealing. Part of the attraction was the commonalities we had, including the shared language and the interactions with Brits we'd met in Uganda. But there was also something about this distant land of opportunities, fairness and decency. It felt like Britain was a distant relative we could visit, a place where things would be better – not only compared to Uganda but also India, a country we associated with poverty and struggle.

On leaving Trafalgar Square, we went by train to Wembley Park (even then a centre for British Asians and a large Jewish community), then by bus to Harrow Road, Wembley. While we were travelling, many English people were kind to us, answering questions about which bus to take, and so on, so our journey gave us a good first impression.

We saw policemen as well. Now, policemen were something we were very wary of. Back home, since Amin came in, they had filled us with fear. But these were just ordinary British bobbies with a cool and calm demeanour. I remember the relief I felt at their professionalism and how good it felt to be fearless in their presence.

We were going to Harrow Road because I had that £200 I'd brought over for a family friend, G. S. Patel. There were foreign exchange controls in most countries at the time and people leaving Uganda were allowed to take out no more than 5,000 shillings – around £200 at the time. I delivered the banker's draft safely as a favour to Patel. This is a very typical thing in the Gujarati community, and I was happy to help, although I think it might be classed as money laundering nowadays!

Patel's brother-in-law owned a post office on Harrow Road; Patel lived above the shop. We found him and gave him his money, and he made us lunch. Real Indian food. Then he rang my brother Manoj. The first job Manoj had found was as a lathe operator in a factory, but he was now working as a bank clerk for Williams & Glyn in central London. When he came to Harrow Road to meet us at the end of the day, his first words were, 'Thank God you are here, I was getting a bit worried.'

Ignatius and I got on a bus with Manoj and went to his digs, which were in Kilburn, at No. 6 Buckley Road. He was living there with my sister Kumud. I remember being amazed on the way there, looking out of the bus window to see white people doing menial tasks, being dustbin men, road menders, and so on. Most of my teachers at Manjasi had been white, highly educated Englishmen, and the way I had pictured white people in Britain was as very middle-class, with degrees and office jobs and all that. It's interesting that the image the British Empire projected, by the time it came to an end, was a middle-class one like that. I guess it was different when there were a lot more soldiers in the colonies.

No. 6 Buckley Road was owned by an Irish family, the Irish still being the dominant immigrant group in Kilburn in those days. I had to give them £6 for them to allow me to stay there. Manoj and Kumud were paying eight. So they put the rent up to fourteen pounds, because we took one extra room. That used up most of the £10 I had brought with me from Uganda, so I would have to get a job pretty sharpish. I had £4 left in the world.

Kumud came home late that evening, about eight o'clock. She was working as a shop assistant. She hugged me and was obviously very pleased to see me; it made me feel very warm, like I had done the right thing in coming to Britain. Kumud had always been a wonderful sister to me, all through my childhood troubles. We ate dal and rice and chapatti that night, there in the Irish house, just like we were at home in Tororo.

The tenor of our conversations that night was, 'OK, we've won the battle, not the war. We eventually need to get the whole family here.' And then Manoj briefed us on going to college – we had to go to Hampstead the next morning.

After breakfast, we got a train from Brondesbury Park to Hampstead Heath. We soon discovered that far from being a proper educational establishment, Woods Tutorial College was, back then, rather impoverished in its vision. There were only two rooms: no books, none of the 'well-equipped laboratories' and other facilities promised in the prospectus. To me, personally, it felt like a con, premised on the basis of getting people into the United Kingdom and squeezing a few quid out of them. It was disgraceful that Manoj's hard-earned cash from the factory had gone on this.

We sat in one of the rooms on hard chairs and after a few minutes a lady in twinset and pearls came in and asked us to write an essay on 'what we thought of this country so far'.

I wrote that many British people had been very kind and helpful, and Ignatius wrote much the same thing. When we were lost, they helped us with detailed directions. But then (so I wrote) we saw British people doing manual work, and that really shocked us: 'Please, no offence, Miss, but look at that white man! He is sweeping the streets!' Because we wouldn't have done that in Uganda. Not us! The Africans would have done that back home. And there was more in this vein. When the woman read it, I think she was quite offended – not about the African part, which was of course the most likely to cause offence, but at the idea that we had collapsed the British system into one homogenous mass.

In her posh, cracked voice, she began to speak words that she thought of as educating us: 'In Britain there are many different walks of life. There are working-class people, middle-class people and upper-class people.'

We didn't really get it. In Uganda, a race system existed, not a class system. This was part of Amin's appeal, that he was going to sweep it all away, making Obote's policy of Africanisation a brutal reality. He really thought of himself as someone fighting apartheid or as one of those Black Panthers in the US. These intentions were correct in some sense (as they were in post-Mandela South Africa) but economically and politically it was a disaster – and morally, too. You can't just chuck 80,000 people out without it having an effect on the whole moral texture of the country. But the tribal favouritism with which Amin replaced the race system, often in conditions of horrific bloodshed, was much worse.

Our so-called classes that day at Woods began then: English and Maths, continuing until three o'clock. Manoj had told us that if we wanted to get work we would have to get a National Insurance number. So we went straight away to a government office and got one.

They gave the NI number to us straight away – none of the palaver about ID that we have now. The thinking in those days was, 'You want to work? Great, here's the form, get on with it, more tax revenue for the government.' The UK needs to be more like that again if it is to get back on its feet economically in the wake of Brexit, not just by creating jobs, but making it really easy for people to be employed. If you come here legally, integrate and work hard, then good luck to you. If you want to come here and bring your own inflexible value system, do not work and rely on welfare, then you don't deserve to live in this great country.

After getting the NI form we got the train back to Kilburn. The next afternoon, after another day in the fake college, I was walking from Brondesbury Tube station back to Buckley Road when I passed a Wimpy burger bar. There was a sign in the window: 'Staff required.'

Ignatius wasn't with me that day; he'd moved in with his cousin, and after that I used to see him outside of college only at the weekend. He'd got himself a job as a dish-washer at an Italian restaurant on Kilburn High Road and travelled daily on the number 28 bus from Fulham. We'd meet on Sunday mornings, either for breakfast or a walk in Hyde Park.

Typical Ignatius, he got himself an English girlfriend while still trying to help Roma get into the country. One day, after Roma had arrived in Britain, she appeared with him in Hyde Park for our walk. Her thunderous face indicated she'd uncovered everything! I don't think she's forgiven Ignatius, nearly fifty years later. But these things happen.

So I went into the Wimpy and filled the form out for a waiting job. A Jewish father and son interviewed me at once, for twenty minutes, in an office out the back. They ran four branches of Wimpy on a franchise basis. Two in Kilburn, one in Wood Green and one in Holloway.

I got the job. They asked me, 'When can you start?'

I said, 'I'll start now! Can I go home and tell my brother?'

So I went back to Buckley Road, but there was nobody there to tell my good news to. My brother came home from work at six and I told him then. So off I went to work in the Wimpy that night, at a rate of twenty-five pence an hour. I remember walking down Kilburn High Road, with my short-sleeved shirt and drainpipe trousers, feeling so happy. I somehow knew I had got the new start in life I'd been looking for.

It was still a shock, though, the exceptional gift of that job, the six o'clock-until-midnight shift, serving Wimpy burgers and chips on brown wooden trays. I'd never seen anything like that before.

Most of the trade consisted of Irish builders. They left their sites, went to the pub, got pissed, and at about ten thirty decided they were hungry and came in for a Wimpy.

Customers who were drunk or at best half-drunk sounds bad, but actually it helped me to engage more, which meant I integrated quicker. My English improved through chatting with them and my confidence grew. They were very warm, those Irish navvies, and (alcohol excepted) some of their culture was very similar to ours. They were family people and would come with their families at weekends; knickerbocker glory and all that for little Liam and Donal.

There was a bit of racism, too. 'Come here, you Paki!' and so on. But in their heart of hearts, they're not racist, the Irish. I remember I told one of them, 'If I'm a Paki, then you're a Paki Paddy.' The whole restaurant burst out laughing, including the man who'd called me a Paki. Mostly they just called me John; when they called me Paki, it was usually because they didn't know my name. I used to tell them, 'Dolar, like an American dollar,' not bothering to explain about the missing 'l'.

So I worked at the Wimpy seven days a week, six to midnight, every day after college, taking food from the grill bar to the tables on plated trays. Saturday was all day, and Sunday was roughly from 11 a.m. to midnight. Friday and Saturday were the heavy days, so that would be a one o'clock finish, maybe, because I had to mop up the floor before I went home.

I got on well with the Jewish owners. The father's English wasn't too good; I think they were probably second generation, from somewhere in central Europe.

I remember one day, after a couple of years or so, by which time McDonald's had launched in Britain, the father called me over and said, 'What do you think about this McDonald's thing?' I didn't know what he was talking about. They explained to me about takeaways in fast-food cartons. I said, 'It'll never work. No British person will eat out of a cardboard box!'

How wrong I was. Now almost all British people have, at one time or another, eaten out of a cardboard box.

I think my business imagination has improved since then, but at the time my ambition was to eventually become a Wimpy manager.

Woods Tutorial College was so useless that I packed it in after three weeks. It was quite a risk as my student visa was due to run out in four months' time. I wrote to the Home Office, explaining what had happened, about the college being a con, me getting a job and so on, adding that I could not return to Uganda because of the licence-to-trade issue and that my father had applied for a voucher. Amazingly, they supported my application and gave me refugee status. In due course, I would apply for naturalisation and, after five years, get a proper UK passport, becoming a British citizen at last.

One day, two good-looking, friendly Indian girls came into the Wimpy. They were from Mombasa (this Kenyan city was, I can tell you, the height of exoticism to any Indian boy brought up in Uganda). We got chatting and after that they used to come regularly, ordering a hamburger without the meat. Just a buttered roll, really. One evening, they told me they went to a college down the road: Kilburn Polytechnic, which was five minutes' walk from the Wimpy. More because I wanted to have more of their company than any great desire for academic success, I told them, 'I also want to go to a proper college,' and then began regaling them with stories about the Woods Tutorial place, which made them laugh. They said, 'Well, why don't you go to Kilburn Poly? They're enrolling for evening classes.'

So I went along to Kilburn Polytechnic, in my innocence, to enrol for the Association of Chartered Certified Accountants (ACCA) qualification. At first I was declined because I didn't have any O levels, but the college officials were very kind to me when I said, using a little creative accounting of my own, that I didn't have any O levels because I had been kicked out of Uganda. I didn't tell them that I had failed all my exams!

I was shown to another desk where they said: 'Well, you can gain O level-equivalent points with an Ordinary National Certificate in business studies.' They added that, with this ONC qualification, I could then do an accountancy qualification and get some exemptions.

So I enrolled myself for the two-year course; the fee was six pounds a year. I went back to the Wimpy and told my bosses that Monday, Tuesday and Wednesday were my college nights now. They were fine with this, letting me come and work during the days and offering me occasional shifts as a chef, which at seventy-five pence an hour paid better than serving food. I earned enough to buy some new clothes, getting myself a plaid shirt and some flared jeans, together with white gym shoes and matching white belt. I started growing my hair longer, too.

As soon as I started at Kilburn Polytechnic, I realised it would be better to get an office job, ideally one in finance. I must have done about forty interviews. Not many people were prepared to employ someone with brown skin in those days. And those places that would employ brown-skinned folk, such as Wimpy, offered limited options in terms of management. I knew I had to start thinking seriously about my career progression.

I settled for extra jobs at clothes shops – first at Bernard Barnes on Kilburn High Road and then at Millets in Wembley. Millets was then a well-known chain, selling jeans, cheesecloth shirts and camping equipment. The manager there, Mr Shaw (he never told me his first name), was Jewish, and the greatest salesman I have ever seen. He would stand outside the front door of the shop with his arms folded and accost anyone who so much as glanced at the window.

'Can I help you, sir?'

'No, I'm just looking.'

'Well, come inside. Let me see if I can help you.'

'No, really, I'm just looking.'

'Do come in, sir. There is no obligation. Please come in. Let me see if I can help you out with something.'

The amount of times I saw Mr Shaw score a success with this tactic was incredible. And having sold them some jeans, he would move on to their need for a shirt.

'No, I'm OK for a shirt, mate, thanks very much.'

'Of course, sir. But let me show you a couple to match the jeans. These Aertex shirts are very fashionable right now, sir, as I am sure you know. Especially these ones in light blue. Look at that – a wonderful match with your jeans.'

Normally, a customer would be there with his wife or girlfriend. 'Yes, it does look nice,' she would agree.

'Absolutely,' Mr Shaw would say. 'Now what about some socks and shoes to go with the outfit?'

I carried on like this for a year, serving and sometimes making food at the Wimpy and learning the tricks of retail sales from Mr Shaw. How he used to woo the window shoppers into the shop and convince to them happily purchase has always stayed with me, teaching me the lesson (still valuable in my role as a government trade envoy) that if you want to trade, you have to sell. I realised later that my English accent and vocabulary had also improved a lot under Mr Shaw's influence.

During this period I also briefly worked for a family-run carpet company called Abagjan. It was a bit of a shambles, that company, and I knew I had to find something more stable. Then one day in June 1972 an employment bureau, Atlas Staff Agency on the Kilburn High Road, got me an interview with a company called United Dominions Trust.

UDT, as it was known, was a finance house in Colindale, NW9. It was one of those old companies associated with imperial leasing and hire purchase, which, since Britain's withdrawal from Empire, had moved more into the domestic market and become a subsidiary of Barclays Bank.

The job was that of audit clerk. First I needed a reference. I went back to my accounts teacher on the business studies course at Kilburn Polytechnic, and he wrote me a nice letter, saying that I was pretty good with figures. (By then this was becoming apparent.)

On the appointed day, I took a number 32 bus from Kilburn to Colindale. The interview at UDT was with a man called Lawrence Archer, who was the company's auditor. In Hyde House, a nine-storey building, he asked me questions like, 'Why are you studying accountancy?'

I said, 'I love numbers.' He went on:

'What other subjects do you do?'

'What time do you go to college?'

'Are you going to continue studying?'

And finally, 'What is your long-term ambition?'

I said to become an accountant. This pleased Mr Archer well enough, as he was an accountant himself.

But none of my answers were why I got the job. It was because of financial measures introduced by the then Chancellor of the Exchequer, Anthony Barber. These involved liberalising the banking industry and establishing a minimum reserve ratio (the portion of cash that commercial banks must hold onto, rather than lend out or invest). He also replaced Purchase Tax and Selective Employment Tax with Value Added Tax (VAT), and relaxed exchange controls; all were prerequisites to membership of the European Economic Community. Barber's measures had led to a mini boom (a bit like the one that would follow in the mid-1980s, after the Big Bang) and a great deal of lending, much of it for property speculation. There was also full employment at the time, more or less. Basically, after years of being in the doldrums, banks and finance companies were run off their feet and needed numerate staff.

This was the beginning of the modern credit industry, as we know it today, for better and worse. It was also the time of the first moves from typewriters to computers, so they needed flexible young minds. My job was to reconcile customers' accounts, finding out where money had gone when it was wrongly posted. For instance, if the customer reference number was 1029 and it had been posted to 1092, I'd go and look at the entries for 1092 and if there was excess, move it back to account 1029.

I sat mainly with a bunch of middle-aged Englishwomen and was pretty lonely, my baby face not exactly helping me to fit in. There was the usual tacit racism, but I didn't mind, really, feeling I was lucky to be there at all. It was not easy to make friends, and I became a smoker to be able to hang out more with members of staff who were my own age. I know very well about all the bad effects of smoking, but the social effect of it, at that time for me, was like being born again: I was no longer the outcast, but part of an active, quintessentially British social dynamic.

All this happened in the first year after I left Uganda. When I look back, it seems astonishing that my life could have changed so much in so short a time, and so clearly for the better. It was a very exciting phase. I was learning to get over my insecurities and to look forward rather than back. I was taking my time to mature, I suppose, slowly releasing my psyche from forms of familial, ethnic and social control; literally, becoming an individual.

But back in Uganda, where my parents were still living, things were getting much worse.

3

THE UGANDAN ASIANS AND
THEIR EXPULSION

In the eighteenth and nineteenth centuries, long before my departure from Uganda in May 1971 and the expulsion of Ugandan Asians the following year, Indians – usually Punjabis – started moving to east Africa, some as independent traders, some as labourers on British imperial schemes, such as the Mombasa–Kampala railway. My own family was part of the vast diaspora from the western Indian state of Gujarat. Although the imperial labour schemes were specific, sometimes involving oppressive indentures that kept a man linked to a project for decades, this pattern of movement was part of a wider and much older picture of monsoon-driven trade to and along the east African coast. Stretching back over a millennium, this saw people from Arabia as well as the Indian subcontinent interacting on a range of levels with people from Africa. As we know, slavery was a very significant part of this picture, but it wasn't the only dimension by any means.

By the eighteenth century, Gujarati traders were moving goods and currency in large quantities up and down the African seaboard and across the Indian Ocean. They were as adept in handling palm oil or sisal as they were in dealing in iron and ivory, and were as happy to take a Maria Theresa thaler as a British Indian rupee.

The usage of the Indian rupee in east Africa extended from Somalia in the north to as far south as Natal in South Africa. In Kenya and Uganda, the British East Africa Company minted their own rupees. The thaler was found throughout east Africa and the Arab world, as accepted in Muscat as it was in Addis Ababa, Bombay and Lourenço Marques. I mention it because 'thaler' gave rise to *daalder* (in Dutch) and *daler* (in Scandinavian languages), which in English became 'dollar'!

Gujaratis weren't only successful in Uganda and other parts of east Africa. They have made their mark across the world, especially in business fields. An article in *The Economist* has called us 'the world's best business people'. A Bangladeshi guy I know takes a more sarcastic view, saying, 'There is only one thing more widespread than the Gujarati and that is the potato.'

Mass emigration from Gujarat, primarily to Africa, began in the 1860s and continued apace until the late 1960s, with the cities of Surat and Porbandar being key departure sites.

There is an old Gujarati proverb to the effect that Gujaratis will prosper wherever they settle. One reason for this is that, despite their mobility, Gujaratis retain links with their community, often across long distances and long periods of time; Gujaratis always pull together. The root of much of this communal energy can be found far back in history, in organisations known as *mahajans*, medieval mercantile guilds set up in the tenth century. They were connected to the development of the *Lohana*, who, in the Hindu caste system, are the merchant class. *Lohanas* are natural-born entrepreneurs. Though most Gujaratis are (well, I am at least) beyond caste divisions, positive aspects of the *Lohana* identity are still going strong, driving an international community based on social clubs and *mahajans* located all over the world. I have been involved with the Global Lohana Convention, which aims to bring members of these clubs and guilds together, with the goal of getting more people involved collectively in philanthropy and education.

Typically, early emigrant Gujaratis to Africa would arrive by dhow in Zanzibar and go from there into the African interior, opening up shops that became known as *dukas*. Key figures in this period in east and central Africa were Allidina Visram (1851–1916) and Vithaldas Haridas (born in 1875). The latter cut through miles of jungle to the small town of Iganga, where he started his own shop. More followed, such as Muljibhai Madhvani (1894–1958), who after working for Haridas would set up in Uganda what became the Madhvani Group. A figure of equivalent importance was Nanjibhai Kalidas Mehta (1887–1969), who founded the Mehta Group of companies in Uganda. Friends as well as competitors, Madhvani and Mehta and their respective children basically built the industrial base of modern Uganda.

With money in their hands to buy with and goods in their storehouses to sell, Gujaratis of successive generations were integral to the developing Ugandan economy. They became the commercial backbone of the country, as Winston Churchill recognised when he visited Uganda as Under-Secretary of State for the Colonies in 1907.

Famously describing Uganda as 'the pearl of Africa', Churchill went on to say:

It is the Indian trader who, penetrating and maintaining himself in all sorts of places to which no white man would go, or in which no white man could earn a living, has more than anyone else developed the early beginnings of trade and opened up the first slender means of communication. It was by Indian labour that the one vital railway on which everything else depends was constructed. It is the Indian banker who supplies perhaps the largest part of the capital yet available for business and enterprise, and to whom the white settlers have not hesitated to recur for financial aid.[2]

The true achievement of those early trader-bankers – in particular people such as Visram, whose multinational enterprise in cotton, sugar, rubber, tea, shipping and currency exchange grew to an enormous size – has not yet really been rescued from history. It would make a good PhD project for someone.

One company alone, the Madhvani Group, accounted for 12 per cent of Uganda's national output, and many other firms excelled. Uganda was granted independence in 1962, and the Ugandan Asians set about working with the government to build the economy further, including constructing schools and hospitals. Yet, as all readers will now know, things did not progress smoothly.

The first signs of trouble involved numerous statements made during 1971 by members of the Ugandan and affiliated journalists about the role of the Asian community in Uganda. Statements calling for a war of economic liberation, getting rid of Asian crooks and exploiters, and such like. The frequency and intensity of these statements, which were full of racial slurs and false accusations, had increased after the coup in January that year, coming at the same

<hr>

2   Winston Churchill, *My African Journey* (London: Hodder & Stoughton, 1908).

time as news of Amin's ethnic killings began to leak out in the international press.

Another sign of things to come was the special Asian Census in October 1971, for which all Ugandan Asians, wherever they were living in the world, had to be present in Uganda to be counted. The administrative outcome of this was fearfully reminiscent of what happened in apartheid South Africa and other countries, as Asian leaders would later point out in a communication to Amin:

> Finally, we would be failing in our duty if we did not inform Your Excellency of the resentment and revulsion felt by Ugandan Asians at the practice of requiring them to carry and produce the Asian Census receipts at the airports and border posts before they are permitted to leave or enter Uganda. We consider this practice is racially discriminatory and reminds one of the system of *kipande* [identity cards – originally pieces of wood painted with a name and number] which was introduced during Colonial times in Kenya and the system of passes now in force in the Apartheid Regime of South Africa ... If such a practice is allowed to continue in Uganda it would be difficult for our leaders to condemn South Africa, Rhodesia and the Portuguese Colonies for indulging in similar discriminatory practices.[3]

The leaders did not make the comparison with Nazi Germany, not least because during this period Amin himself had been making wild statements that cited his approval for what Hitler did to the

---

3 Hasu Patel, 'General Amin and the Indian Exodus from Uganda', *Issue*, vol. 2, no. 4, p.15.

Jews. Amin's words had sparked outrage in the world's press, but for Ugandan Asians the issue was anything but rhetorical.

Next, fatefully, Amin called for an 'Indian conference' to be held on 7–8 December 1971 at the International Conference Centre in Kampala. This had the effect of bringing the Asian community in Uganda – Hindus, Muslims and Goans (who were mainly Catholic, like Ignatius) – together to save their putative future role in the country. In the first memorandum presented to the conference, the Asian communities voiced the hope that it would bring a new phase of cordial relations between Africans and Asians in Uganda. They also detailed a generalised Asian view on a variety of topics: social integration (pointing to the Asian role in service organisations, such as the Lions Club, and outlining difficulties with interracial marriage); education; citizenship and immigration; trade and commerce; and the Asian contribution to economic development in the produce-processing industries, engineering, financial organisations, retail and the professional cadres of the civil service. Asians were key to many of these areas of Ugandan life.

Amin sent his Defence Minister, Charles Oboth Ofumbi, to attend the first day of the conference, but the Asians' arguments fell on deaf ears. (Serving as Defence Minister until 1973, Oboth Ofumbi would die in 1977 while awaiting trial for his part in an alleged coup attempt against Amin. It is generally accepted that he was murdered under the orders of the General, although the official account is of a car accident. Archbishop Janani Luwum, who had spoken out against Amin in sermons, and land minister Lieutenant Colonel Erinayo Oryema were killed in the same incident.)

On the second day of the conference, Amin himself appeared. He proceeded to launch a series of broadsides against Asians in

Uganda, at the same time as continuing to present himself as the national 'father of the family', and acknowledging that the colonial legacy was in part to blame for the lack of integration. He did say, 'No one doubts the various positive contributions which you Asians have made since the arrival of your forefathers in east Africa as railway builders,' but the insulting tone with which he spoke was merely a preamble for a full-scale attack on the Asian community.

Amin lambasted Asians for living in the past and keeping Africans below them. He attacked them for: commercial malpractice (including keeping two sets of accounts and unclear pricing of goods); illegal repatriation of foreign exchange; smuggling across borders; hoarding to create artificial shortages; the offering of bribes for licences and permits; and passport irregularities.

On citizenship, Amin declared that commitments entered into by the previous government were legally binding; thus citizenship certificates properly issued before 25 January 1971 would be honoured. His government was not bound, however, to process any outstanding claims for citizenship, and these were automatically cancelled. Fresh application would have to be made in the future. In any case, the government was disturbed at the lack of faith shown in Uganda, for the majority of Indians had refused Ugandan citizenship when offered it after independence. This sad state of affairs was highlighted by the fact that within a single family, two individuals might have different nationalities.

Amin also spoke of disloyalty (he gave the example of Ugandan Asian doctors and lawyers training in Uganda but practising abroad) and of lack of integration. He singled out the rarity of marriages between Asian women and Ugandan men (saying that there had only been six, to his knowledge) while adding that it was not unusual to find Asian men living with Ugandan women. He said that he supported this 'living and loving with African girls … as it pointed the way to integration between Africans and Asians,' but added that Asian parents tended to react negatively to it, imposing 'social restrictions that are completely out-of-date'.

More or less, Amin laid all of the problems relating to the relationship between the Asians and Africans in Uganda at the door of the Asians, saying, 'It is you yourselves, through your refusal to integrate with the Africans in this country, who have created this feeling towards you by the Africans.'

Unsurprisingly, these remarks threw the now-united Asian community into confusion, giving a new political reality to the vilifications that had been appearing in the press. The Asian leaders produced a second memorandum, trying to answer some of the charges, but it was all to no avail. Various other dialogues took place in the following months, but all were equally fruitless.

The next phase in the story took place in Tororo, my adoptive hometown, fifteen months after I had left the country. On 4 August 1972, while travelling south from Karamoja, President Amin addressed the officers and men of the Airborne Regiment that was stationed there, under the Tororo Rock that had dominated the landscape of my childhood. In a rambling speech, Amin told the troops that he'd had a dream in which God had told him to expel the Asians, saying that Uganda had no place 'for the over 80,000 Asians holding British passports who are sabotaging Uganda's economy and encouraging corruption,' adding that he wanted to see Uganda's economy in the hands of black Ugandans.

Characteristically, while recounting his divine dream in Tororo, Amin got his figures wrong. There were in fact some 70,000 Asians in Uganda, but only about 30,000 of these were British passport holders. The remainder held Ugandan citizenship (23,242), or held Indian, Pakistani, Bangladeshi, Kenyan or Tanzanian passports (4,758). The remaining 12,000 were effectively stateless, having made applications for Ugandan citizenship that, long delayed, were now summarily cancelled by the regime.

Amin chaotically altered his rulings in the succeeding months, sometimes referring to 'some Asians', at other times 'many Asians' and often simply 'Asians'. All this added to the confusion, and the feeling that there was nothing to be done but to leave.

The key issue in law was whether Asians with Ugandan citizenship could be expelled or not. The Ugandan Chief Justice, Ben Kiwanuka, told Amin he could not expel Asians who held Ugandan nationality.

As with that of Oboth Ofumbi and Archbishop Luwum, Kiwanuka's fate was a sobering demonstration of the character of the man Uganda was dealing with – *all* Ugandans, not just Ugandan Asians. In the immediate aftermath of an abortive counter-coup by Obote in 1972, Kiwanuka was arrested at gunpoint by Amin's men as he presided over a session of Uganda's High Court. As well as countermanding from the bench other of Amin's more draconian orders besides the one relating to the expulsion, Kiwanuka had also secretly agreed to support Obote's attempts to return to power.

Kiwanuka was killed by Amin's forces on 22 September 1972, at Makindye Military Prison. The prolonged execution, according to eyewitnesses, involved Kiwanuka's ears, nose, lips and arms being severed from his body, followed by disembowelling and castration before, finally, he was immolated.[4]

---

4   David Martin, *General Amin* (London: Faber & Faber, 1974).

The expulsion was a turbulent business. In terms of institutional government administration, from which to an extent Amin's public ravings were separate, the technicalities became tortuous, details and stipulations ramifying as the process developed. Technically, only the British Asians were expelled at first, leaving the rest to stay. This then progressed to cover all Indian, Pakistani and Bangladeshi nationals, and finally *all* Asians. Fewer than fifty elected to stay, toughing it out through decades of brutal treatment. Notable among these were members of the family of my good friend Sanjay Tanna, who would later become an MP in a different, better Uganda.

Nearly everyone else fled. Luckily for me and for them, my parents and my siblings left Uganda just before things became critical. My sister Sumitra came to England in October 1971, and my parents and three remaining brothers, Pankaj, Kantesh and Suresh, came in March 1972.

Under Amin's maliciously intolerant rule (he went on to murder and torture hundreds of thousands of his own people), those with British, Indian or other non-Ugandan passports (and sometimes none at all) were forced to leave behind everything, taking with them literally just the clothes on their backs. Brutally evicted, they were given only three months to leave. On the television in Britain, my family and I watched people's baggage being opened on the tarmac; we watched jewellery and watches being taken off people (some of whom we recognised) as they fled to waiting planes. It was awful. We felt oddly guilty about having got out earlier, but also, retrospectively, a huge sense of relief.

Most of those expelled were poor traders like my father. But some of those who had to leave were very big players, commercially and politically speaking. My dear friend and mentor, as he would become, Manubhai Madhvani, was in the latter category. I want to tell Manubhai's story, because he became an important figure in the Ugandan–Asian community in Britain and, to a lesser extent, in the Arabian Gulf.

Manubhai's father, Muljibhai, started trading in Uganda in 1914, sixteen years before Manubhai was born. Manubhai joined his older brother, the charismatic businessman and politician Jayant-bhai, in the family home in Jinja in 1930, having spent his teens in Bombay (where he had listened to and been inspired by Gandhi). On joining the family sugar cane business, Manubhai showed a keen entrepreneurial flair that, coupled with his life-long ability to remain courteous, kind and infinitely polite, made him an invaluable asset.

The sad loss of Manubhai's father in 1958 was then followed by the untimely death of his brother Jayantbhai, two events that suddenly promoted Manubhai to a position of great responsibility in the family, at a time of growing uncertainty in Uganda (the same uncertainty my own family was feeling, but on a much larger scale commercially). Although this unanticipated role (and the commercial environment) was daunting, Manubhai worked with his other brothers to grow the family business and, eventually, the Madhvani Group was one of the largest companies in east Africa.

Manubhai became one of the wealthiest and most prominent Asians in the country, and because of this status he was imprisoned by Amin in the infamous Singapore Block of Makindye Prison, the same place in which Kiwanuka was murdered. On his release, Manubhai fled to England, a country that, like me, he was proud to adopt as his home.

The expulsion led to a global game of political football. India claimed the expelled Asians were the British government's responsibility. Kenya and Tanzania closed their borders to them once it became apparent there would be a flood of new immigrants. In England, advertisements in Leicester (which had become a magnet for refugees) warned Ugandans not to go there as there was now no housing and no jobs. People ended up as far afield as Canada, India, Australia, the US and many other places, with both family and friends being separated. Those without established statehood left as UN refugees, with many simply driving over the porous border to Kenya.

There was a terrible moment here in Britain when Parliament, having been stung by its experience of larger-than-expected numbers of Asian immigrants from Kenya in the preceding four years, hesitated before actually agreeing to allow the Ugandan Asians to come.

Yet the Conservative Prime Minister, Edward Heath, and his government rose above the rhetoric of Enoch Powell and others, and demonstrated the compassion that I have come to associate with Britain. Heath ruled that Britain had a legal and moral responsibility to take in those with British passports, saying, 'This is our duty. There can be no equivocation. These are British subjects with British passports. They are being expelled from their country, which in many cases is the land of their birth. They are entitled to come here and they will be welcome here.'

Between August and November 1972, around 28,000 refugees, comprising around 8,000 families, arrived homeless and scared at Stansted Airport (in those days not much more than a few hangars). Another couple of thousand, including Manubhai Madhvani, came through Heathrow. In an age when flights are now so regular, it is difficult to appreciate how organised the British had to be to ferry so many people across two continents in just ninety days. The smooth and successful operation stands as a great testament to those involved and to British organisation in general. The Ugandans were greeted at Stansted and Heathrow by a large number of charitable and voluntary organisations which gave them food and shelter.

The then Home Secretary, Robert Carr, established the Uganda Resettlement Board and sixteen temporary camps were set up across the country on old military bases, many of which were in East Anglia. The resettlement committee did fantastic work and we British Asians remain very grateful to them, including Praful Patel, who was the board's sole Asian member.

It was obviously a very difficult time for the newly arrived, most of whom were traumatised and penniless. Some encountered racial discrimination on arrival, jobs were not always plentiful and initially life was often tough: long hours in low-paid employment and living in cramped and sometimes squalid accommodation.

It is hard for many of the younger members of the east African Indian community in Britain to understand what their parents and grandparents faced. Many who came to Britain had never asked for handouts in their lives, yet they had arrived with literally nothing.

The political opposition to the influx continued, including from some quarters of the Tories. Enoch Powell tried to get through a motion at the Conservative Party conference condemning the policy of acceptance. But opposition from the Young Conservatives and the Federation of Conservative Students saw the motion defeated by 1,721 votes to 736.

In Leicester, which took an initial allotment of around 7,000 Asians, the local National Front encouraged whites to protest. But after a brief burst of ugly support, the mass of right-minded British citizens, together with the police and local media, kept the fascists in check. And thank God they did – not least because these Asians, fleeing discrimination at home and now potentially facing it in exile, would end up saving Leicester's economy. They developed food and clothing enterprises, as well as other businesses; by 2002, Ugandan Asians had created 30,000 jobs in Leicester and represented 11 per cent of the city's employers.

The wonderful thing is that Leicester now welcomes immigrants from countries in Africa other than Uganda. I remember doing a radio interview in Leicester in around 2013 that was broadcast to the city's Somali community, which has grown substantially in recent years. I was asked for my opinion on why the British Indian community had been a success and said that it was down to one thing: integration.

The resentment we sometimes felt after we had first arrived made us stronger and even more determined to integrate ourselves, and today it is clear that Uganda's loss is very much Britain's gain. But at the time, such a degree of future success was unimaginable.

I still remember the determination of our community leaders to celebrate Diwali here in Britain, even though many of the exiled people barely had a roof over their heads. But this did not stop people from hiring church halls and the like to conduct our ceremonies.

And of course there were also many warm welcomes to balance the opposition we faced. As my British Gujarati friend Lord Parekh was later to remark:

ABOVE An anxious-looking Dolar in the playground of Rock View School in 1968, with Tororo Rock in the background.

LEFT A young Dolar exploring Hyde Park upon his arrival in London from Uganda in 1971.

LEFT Dolar outside Kilburn Polytechnic in 1973, where it all began.

BELOW Rockware Glass FC, circa 1975; Dolar is fourth from the right.

BOTTOM Dolar and Sandhya's civil marriage at Hendon Registry Office, Barnet, in 1980.

LEFT The happy couple on their honeymoon in Calgary, Alberta.

BELOW Dolar introducing Margaret Thatcher to key members of the British Indian community in Finchley.

BOTTOM Three generations from three different worlds: Dolar, his parents and his eldest son, Rupeen, who was just a year old.

Sandhya welcoming John Major with a traditional Indian garland to the Popats' home for a reception, just weeks before Major became Prime Minister.

Dolar's three sons, Shivaan, Paavan and Rupeen, at their new home, The Knoll, in Stanmore.

Dolar's new office in Harrow, which would be his business base for years to come.

It is very striking that this was more or less the first time since the Second World War that ordinary British people had offered their homes and hospitality to people whom they had never seen, as they did with the Ugandan Asians. In the first three months, 2,000 private individuals had offered their homes, and within about a year that figure had risen to 5,000.[5]

Even some politicians opened their homes to Ugandan Asians, including Conservative MP Peter Bottomley and his wife Virginia, later Secretary of State for Health in John Major's government and now Baroness Bottomley, sitting on the same red benches as me in the House of Lords. Meanwhile in Leicester, where there had been so much worry about a flood of immigrants, the council created an environment for Ugandan Asians in which they could prosper, showing a particularly wise handling of immigration.

I have mentioned that families were sometimes split up, with people going their separate ways to Canada, Australia, the United States or India, rather than all coming to England. Although difficult at the time, this has meant that extended families have over the intervening period formed both support and commercial networks. This has proved to be an important factor in the wider success of Ugandan Asians, as it was with the Jews before them.

I want to say a few words about that connection. When the British Indian community – particularly those of us who were viciously evicted from east Africa – arrived in England, we were penniless, somewhat downhearted and in need of inspiration. Much came

---

5   Hansard, HL Deb, 6 December 2012, vol. 741, col. 806.

in the form of the Jewish community: where they led, we have followed.

Many of us recognised that, like us, members of the Jewish community had arrived in this country with nothing, and were also the victims of prejudice. Yet, we knew that Jews had succeeded in building a better life for themselves and their families in Britain.

Over the past forty years it has become clear that the British Indian and Jewish communities have much in common. We share the same values: aspiration; hard work; a belief in enterprise; a dedication to education; the importance of faith, family, philanthropy and community; and, perhaps most crucial of all, the importance of integrating into wider society.

Wembley, where I had settled, and neighbouring Harrow, where I was to settle later, already had a very substantial Jewish community, some of the members of which had come as a result of an earlier exile, the *Kindertransport* – the children who had fled Nazi Germany. Along with local Harrow MP Hugh Dykes (whom I would later work with closely when I got into local politics), Edward Heath identified Harrow as a suitable place for Ugandan Asians to settle.

So, I was no longer a rarity. Harrow, Wembley, Southall: all these places began filling up with commercially-minded but shell-shocked Asians keen to make their way, all very grateful to Britain (as I was) to have found a berth. As for my first house in Wembley, I soon had twenty-five people living there, many of them relatives from Uganda: my siblings and parents and various cousins and uncles, all cramped up together in three bedrooms and two reception rooms. As time went on, people eventually moved to their own rental places.

After the expulsion of Asians from Uganda, and as a result of difficult conditions in other African countries, a further wave of migration in the 1970s brought Gujaratis to (again, principally) England, Canada and the United States. These people also began by focusing on business, many setting up corner shops or running sub-post offices, as I did. Because Gujaratis have a strong foundation in commerce, there was a sense that a shop couldn't fail.

But the younger generation of arrivals diversified into white-collar jobs, such as accountancy, engineering and medicine. This gave rise to the joke, 'What is an Indian without a shop?' 'A doctor.'

Many Gujaratis also became pharmacists. Gujaratis probably own more independent pharmacies in Britain and the United States than any other ethnic group. They run about half the independent pharmacies in the US and astonishingly a third of its small hotels and motels; Americans describe this as the 'Hotel, Patel and Motel' phenomenon (similar to how we British Indians used to be teased about all being the owners of a corner shop!). A quarter of Silicon Valley start-ups are believed to have Gujarati links. Gujaratis are also very active in the world diamond business. In Britain, figures such as Shriti Vadera and Jitesh Gadhia – who are also Ugandan Asians – have distinguished themselves in both banking and politics (both are now members of the House of Lords).

Beyond these fields, there are very big Gujarati conglomerates that originated in India, such as Reliance, which is owned by the Ambani brothers. These kinds of enterprises benefited from a general increase in economic activity in India that began in the late 1980s and has continued ever since.

Hard work, education, enterprise and family were the hallmark values of most British Gujaratis of east African origin. Our success relates to aspiration and ambition, to an attitude based on getting on and going up, making some money, keeping our family in health and comfort, and having our children do better in life than we have.

We didn't want to be working class, but middle class. This is precisely what most British people are or want to be. Having been at the bottom, we had a dream of being at the top, and we were willing to work together to make that happen.

4

CARRYING ON REGARDLESS

In the midst of the exodus of Asians from Uganda to Britain in 1972, the trauma of which was tempered only by the joy of seeing old friends and close relatives, I continued working as an audit clerk at United Dominions Trust. I must have been pretty good at my job, because after four months Lawrence Archer promoted me, saying that he liked the forensic attitude I took in sorting out the discrepancies between accounts.

While I was at UDT, aged eighteen, I bought my first house: 130 Tokyngton Avenue in Wembley. Manoj and I, and my two sisters Sumitra and Kumud, cobbled together the savings we had to pay the deposit. I used a broker and paid him £150, and he got me a mortgage. I didn't know how he'd done it at the time, but I later found out that he had put on the application form that I was a car salesman. That kind of thing happened a lot in those days. Anyway, I got a mortgage of £8,500 from the Abbey National Building Society in Shepherd's Bush.

For a lot of Englishmen, their home is their castle and they have a strong emotional connection with their property; for Gujaratis in Britain then, a house was about finance and security. We tend not to like renting because it is just money lost, and it was difficult for us to rent nice places in those days because of our skin colour. But buying this house was also about the security of moving to a better area in London and having our own roof over our heads, and we knew our parents were likely to join us in London before long.

That year, I was invited to the UDT Christmas party. It was a lavish affair with nearly 1,000 attendees, and it was the first time I'd ever had to wear black tie. The event was held in Watford, but I felt so out of place it may as well have been on Mars. I remember finding one other Indian guy at the party, the boyfriend of one of the attendees. Ricki Tailor was his name, and we chatted for hours that night. He's still a close friend all these years later.

Despite the promotion, I only stayed another six months at UDT, as I had realised that I would be better placed doing accountancy in a factory environment. I also didn't like the department I had been promoted to, as I was having to start the frightening process of integrating myself as a coloured person among whites all over again. I didn't feel I belonged at UDT. I was the only coloured guy there and, although the women I worked with were tolerant to a point, it was obvious that there was always going to be some segregation, through ignorance as much as anything else.

The accountancy lecturer at Kilburn Polytechnic had advised me that if I worked for a manufacturing company, I could become eligible for sponsored membership of the Institute of Cost and Works Accountants (ICWA). Now called the Chartered Institute of Management Accountants, this was more open than the other qualifying body, the Association of Chartered Certified Accountants, which I had initially been working towards.

My aspirations were taking shape. I wanted to get myself into the ivory tower of qualified accountants. So I moved from UDT to a firm that made signs at a site in north-west London. Sign Brite had around 120 staff. I worked there as a cost clerk, costing out the profit implications for the various enquiries they received, which were mainly about making the signs for petrol stations.

But again, this was a family company, run by two brothers; working there I saw a lot of the kind of arguments that I would later try to avoid when I had my own family-run companies. These two brothers were white, working-class Londoners who'd set up their own business. They were doing quite well but running the company as if it were still just the two of them. Even their wives would come into the office and shout at each other! The older brother was extremely hard working and technically minded. The younger was more laid back, but a good salesman. (Quite a typical division between brothers working together in their own business.) The younger brother was more flamboyant, taking money out of petty cash, and then the older one would come and ask me, 'What was that money for?', and I'd have to try to account for it all. When you're a small firm of 100-plus staff, you've got to professionalise. You can't keep running the business the same way you did when you started.

Throughout my time with Abadjan, UDT and Sign Brite, I was still working shifts at the Wimpy. On Friday, Saturday and Sunday evenings, I'd find myself back among the well-oiled Celtic customers. Quite a shift of gear.

My next big break came at a company called Rockware Glass, where in late summer 1973 I gained employment as a trainee accountant. They made beer and milk bottles at factories in St Helens, Liverpool, Knottingley and Doncaster. I was by now about to finish my ONC in business studies and looking to begin a 'proper' accountancy qualification, as discussed with my lecturer. My other jobs at Abadjan, UDT and Sign Brite had all turned out to be false starts in the sense of setting me on the right road. But with each one it wasn't like I had a choice but to take the position – there weren't any other options available.

Rockware agreed to give me day release to study to be a chartered management accountant – or, as it used to be called, a 'cost and works' accountant – at Harrow Technical College (later University of Westminster). Two of the trained accountants at Rockware, Malcolm Kneill and John Cole, helped me get student membership of the ICWA, with John being the signatory on my application form. As an associate member of the Institute, John was able to recommend other people for membership. It was a big help, someone saying, 'Smart bloke – hasn't got O levels but awaiting results from ONC in business studies and working with us.' To my eternal surprise, my membership application was accepted.

I knew instantly that this was my big break. The rules made it clear that I shouldn't have got in, as you needed a minimum of five O levels to be accepted. Yet John Cole's endorsement was enough to open the door, and that was all I needed. Without that act of kindness, I simply would never have had the opportunities I've had in my life. It makes me emotional to think how much John's actions at that time changed everything for me.

At Rockware, I was the only coloured guy working in a staff of 400, and perhaps this is why the chairman of the whole company took a shine to me.

His name was Peter Parker. He was a very clever, suave and well-travelled man who had grown up in India and Africa and served in various countries abroad in the Army Intelligence Corps. As well as being chair of Rockware Group, he was at that time on the boards of Bookers Engineering and Industrial Holdings, Associated British Maltsters, Dawnay Day Group and the literary agency Curtis Brown. In 1976, Parker would be appointed chairman of British Rail by the Labour government and would continue to serve in that role during the premiership of Margaret Thatcher, becoming a household name as he dealt with numerous industrial disputes.

These battles would test his socialist principles, but back at Rockware, when I was a youth (and still quite a shy and nervous one in those days), Parker showed a real commitment to equality by taking me under his wing.

It began with me having to do some small task for Rockware's chief financial accountant, Malcolm Kneill (photocopying, or punching figures into a machine), and he asked me to get him a cup of coffee. Malcolm was a nice guy who ended up helping to direct my career. He always wore a crisp white shirt with a small knot tie, and his red-framed glasses caught the eye. He was a hyperactive accountant, never happy sitting behind his desk and always running from one place to another. With eight of us in an office, it was always his all-action approach and gruff accent that dominated.

Then Malcolm asked me to come in one Saturday to help with the directors' loan accounts. I found myself fetching coffee or tea for all the top people in the company. One day, the chairman himself, Parker, shouted across the room, waving a bit of paper: 'Dolar! We've got this wrong! Can you sort it out for us?'

After that, I began getting Parker hot drinks whenever he was in the office after hours and doing a lot more professional work besides, regularly getting paid overtime. Parker himself seemed to work very hard, which I suppose is not surprising as he had that many directorships. He'd come and find me in the course of the ordinary working week, picking me out of the rows of clerical desks, saying, 'Dolar, would you mind doing this for me?'

So I became a sort of executive assistant for one of the top businessmen in the whole country, and I learned a lot. On one occasion, though, I thought I'd gone too far. We were at the Rockware annual general meeting and the directors were busy praising themselves for their 8 per cent increase in profits.

When the floor was opened up to questions, I stood up and said, 'Our profits may be up by 8 per cent, but inflation [public enemy number one at that time] is at 16 per cent, so have we really done that well?' Looking back, I'm amazed I did it. Public speaking was (and is) my biggest fear, and I'd stood up and questioned the directors of the company I worked for. My nerves weren't helped by the glances from my co-workers in the audience. But Peter Parker was delighted I'd asked 'such an important question'. He went on to say how we hoped the Prices and Incomes Policy of the Labour government would help drive down inflation. His warmth towards my question did not go unnoticed by others. Once it became apparent I was his favourite, the prejudice of others evaporated.

For a while, on top of the job at Rockware, I continued working at Wimpy as a waiter and cook, in the evenings on Saturdays and Sundays. Now and then there were fights, with people being so drunk, and everyone would laugh at me when I tried to intervene to stop them. I was still skinny and baby-faced, even though I was nineteen by now. It's a real curse being baby-faced: it automatically makes people think you are vulnerable and not ready to be taken seriously, almost like an invitation to be bullied. It was a curse that would stay with me throughout my early career, especially when I

was running my own finance company, as it meant that businessmen wouldn't want to pay my fees.

So for a period I was living this double life: Peter Parker and
directors' loan accounts in the week and clearing up after brawls in
a Kilburn Wimpy at the weekend (those Irish guys really knew how
to fight; no matter what was thrown at them, they just kept coming
back for more).

But there were odd synchronicities. Effectively being a waiter
again at Rockware, making teas and coffees for the directors, won
me the sort of respect and opportunities to integrate that I could
never have found by other means. Having this special position not
only enabled me to see how these senior figures operated but also
gave me the confidence that, eventually, I would be able to do the
same sort of thing. And you know what, I even learned an important lesson from the Irish labourers back at the Wimpy: not to be
violent, but to stand up again if you got knocked down.

In time, Rockware became a more diverse company. They hired
a well-spoken Anglo-Indian called Rodney and then they hired my
sister, Sumitra. They had realised, I think partly as a result of my
example, that Indians work hard and tend to be good at figures.
They also hired a Nigerian guy, Peter Ogalu. As these other people
from ethnic minorities were hired, I became more integrated
myself, joining one of the company football teams (Finance playing Marketing, for example). These sorts of opportunities are very
important in the journey from immigrant outsider to becoming a
member of your adoptive society. Integration cannot be achieved
through only one single means, least of all legislation – it's part
of a big picture that involves the immigrant immersing himself or
herself at as many levels of social, civic and political life as possible.

5

GOING FAST

In mid-1976, Rockware moved its headquarters from London to Northampton. All members of staff were given a choice: be made redundant or relocate with the company. I chose redundancy, and with the money made a down payment on a second house. I also purchased my first car at this point, a Datsun that I bought for £600.

Peter Parker had recommended me to a chap called Alderman Hartley, who was a Labour councillor for our local constituency, Brent. He was very active in the area, and had previously come to our house to encourage us to vote. We had no idea what he was talking about and thought we had no right to participate in British elections, but he persuaded us that we could, and should.

Brent was a Conservative seat at the time, so Alderman Hartley obviously thought our family would be useful. I remember on one occasion he invited me to a local Residents Association meeting in St Michael's Church, which was near where we lived. There had been a lot of complaints about the number of migrants moving to the area. I was, unsurprisingly, the only Indian present. I took my first dip into political waters and spoke out on behalf of those arriving, trying to explain why they'd come here. But there was no sympathy in the audience – the racism was clearly too ingrained. I never bothered attending again. It only increased my desire to move elsewhere.

In those days, as a social housing measure, Brent Council was allowing mortgages to be supported by more than one income, which meant people could buy houses in groups. We had benefitted from this new rule when we moved from Wembley to Kenton, with our new house being bought with a joint-income mortgage in the names of my two brothers, Manoj and Pankaj. (In 1977 we transferred the mortgage into my name so that I could re-mortgage the property and fund the £5,000 deposit I needed to start my first Post Office business in Watford.)

The value of property was going up quickly, as were rental rates. I became what would be known now as a buy-to-let landlord, as we kept our previous property in Wembley and I rented it out. By this stage Manoj had married, and he and his wife, Illa, had moved to Canada. My wider network of friends and family helped a lot during these deals, all of us sharing equity and borrowing from each other in various ways.

Kenton was a nicer area to move to, and the property had four bedrooms, so was bigger than the Wembley house that we had been in. My parents lived with me and my brothers Pankaj, Suresh and Kantesh, whom I shared a room with. But we were all happy to be together and we rarely spoke of Uganda. It was too scary – at that time we felt as if we would never want to go back.

I had rent from the Wembley property, but I still needed a job to cover all the payments, having spent my Rockware redundancy money on that new car. I quickly secured another job at Sperry Univac. This was an international company that manufactured computers, selling into fourteen different countries. The head offices were in Boston. I was by this stage a part-qualified accountant, having done three of the five parts of my professional qualification as a chartered management accountant.

Sperry was a much more international and diverse company than any I had previously worked at. My boss, Hiro Karam, was an Indian married to an English woman. My job was to process management information, aligning what was happening between all the countries – orders that came in, how much stock had been delivered, how much outstanding work in progress there was. I had to send this information off by telex to the US every week to the chief accountant and directors.

The company also had a very different work ethic to British firms. Americans are quite like Gujaratis: they pay well, but they'll get the most out of you, thinking nothing of calling you at home at twelve o'clock at night (ignoring the effect of the time difference). It was a culture that I felt very comfortable with. So I worked hard, but privately I was focusing on the goal of self-employment and running my own show. It wasn't easy, working towards something of my own while also holding down a full-time job.

I first saw for myself the need for small business finance while trying to raise money to buy my own small business, a sub-post office and corner shop in Watford, which I acquired in 1977.

It was a very typical thing for an Asian family to do in those days, to acquire a post office or a corner shop, then combine in one business a general store and newsagents (newspapers and magazines, confectionery and tobacco). My family had experience of trading in east Africa; we knew that these sorts of shops became central to local communities – thus would guarantee trade, as well as help us to integrate – and as a family-run business we knew there'd be no prejudice among the workforce. It was still difficult for many east Africans to get a job at the time, so having your own business was a real victory. In time, this approach to business would change the nature of local shopping in Britain, opening the door (literally) for longer opening hours.

But I had real trouble raising the money for my sub-post office, going to around forty different banks. No luck. In the end, I was successful with a company called Forward Trust, a finance house that was part of Midland Bank and which were specialists in business lending. Their rates were expensive, but they took the risk because they understood the industry.

I bought the business and soon made it more profitable by extending the shop's opening hours and increasing the turnover of stock. Six months later, with the business now established, I managed to refinance the loan at a much lower rate with a clearing bank, National Westminster (now better known as NatWest). So I learned a very important lesson, which is that to raise money is difficult, but to refinance for the same proposition is much easier.

In 1979, while still running my post office, I set up a firm of accountants called Simon Sternberg, along with a partner of Kenyan Asian extraction, Anil Kotecha. Anil was a friend from Kilburn Poly who had – unlike me – gone on to qualify fully as an accountant. We purposely gave the business a Jewish name because we wanted to attract not only Indians but also people from a range of ethnic communities, and because there was – and still is – a perception that the Jewish community are very successful in business. The name helped to give us a head start by getting customers through the door.

By this stage, I had begun in a small way to help traders in the Asian diaspora get finance. The plan was to draw clients to the accountancy practice by offering to finance their businesses too. The original purpose of the financing side, which I eventually developed, was solely to build up this accountancy practice. But it soon became clear that having used our firm to finance a project, people didn't then tend to appoint us as accountants. They chose somebody else because they wanted to move on from the financing stage. So in fact, in many ways out of frustration, my part of the operation morphed into a finance brokerage service for small businesses.

It was during this time that I began to realise that the art of lending finance was to put yourself in the lender's shoes and present a case to his liking, to his own guidelines and discretion. Bank managers were nervous about sending applications to head office, so in my work as a broker the trick was for me to find a manager who had enough leeway to approve it. Present a watertight case and there's no way they can say no to it. There were lots of people doing this for personal lending, like the broker who arranged my mortgage, but no one was doing it for commercial lending, at least not for small businesses. One of the effects of the Ugandan exodus, and of other migrations from Commonwealth countries, such as Pakistan and Bangladesh, was that there were a lot of traders looking for this kind of service – immigrants who felt adrift in their new country.

These immigrants wanted someone they could go to who was 'one of them'; someone who could work through the language barriers and who understood how urgently they wanted things. Back then, trying to become the owner of a corner shop was difficult; every shop for sale had five buyers ready to go. So these immigrant entrepreneurs needed someone who understood finance, could speak their language and could deliver at speed.

With all this in mind, I parted from Simon Sternberg in 1981, with Anil taking the accountancy part of the business (which he still runs today) and me the finance part. I set up Fast Finance plc, which was the first firm in Britain to specialise in business finance for small businesses. I charged 1 per cent on every deal and I couldn't keep the customers away. This business would provide the main thrust of my activity throughout the 1980s, during which I built on a culture of contacts, many of whom couldn't speak English and were thus particularly appreciative of my services.

The flat above my post office in Watford had three bedrooms. Two were let out and the third was to become the home to Fast Finance. It was a simple set up: a desk in the centre of the room for me, with a couple of filing cabinets against the wall and a corner desk for my new PA, Sarah. She was seventeen, well-spoken and white, which I felt helped to give the firm a more professional image. Straight out of college, Sarah quickly became part of the family.

I called the business Fast Finance because with finance for small businesses, it's very important how quickly you can raise funds – more important than the amount you are raising, in some cases. There was real demand for corner shops, as I have said, mainly from the east African Indians who had flooded into the country. These African Indians worked harder than other people. With extended hours and a wider range of stock, they often doubled their turnover in a matter of months, so they were quickly in a position to raise more funds and to buy more goods to sell, or other properties, or to refinance their existing deals.

The usual process for someone hoping to get a loan would be

to see their bank manager, and they'd get the inevitable 'There's an appointment next Tuesday morning'-type response, with further delays and bureaucracy to come. My work was to circumnavigate this process. A client would get an appointment through Sarah, I'd see them either that same day or the next and, based on their situation, put together the most appropriate proposal in a package for the bank. I always wanted those packages ready within forty-eight hours of meeting a client and I would drive the paperwork over to whichever bank branch was most suitable. My reputation among the bank managers meant that none of my clients were ever interviewed.

On my desk at Fast Finance there were two phones, so that when a client rang with a query I'd be able to keep them holding on one line while I phoned the bank or the solicitors on another. Business-es hate delays and I wanted to streamline all of our work. It was pretty adrenaline-filled, and I drank a lot of coffee to power myself through the day. The work was non-stop. I had a line connected to the shop downstairs and when it got busy I'd be down there doing shifts. Perhaps the only time we slowed down was on Friday afternoons, when we'd get fish and chips from Bert Longman's shop just up the road.

There's another reason I called the business Fast Finance: be-cause everything I do in life is fast. That's just my nature. I can't wait for things to happen. Of course, I have learned to moderate myself, up to a point. When I play golf my old impatience comes flowing out, which is a disaster for my game. It's left to my children to tell me to 'slow down, enjoy it'.

I got married in 1980, which happened quite quickly, too. My wife, Sandhya, is the daughter of Hansaben and Jamnadasbhai

Lukka. Hansaben was a kind woman from a very large family. She had a captivating quality that made conversations with her really enjoyable, and she was also very artistic and creative. Her house was the family head office. All her relatives would gather there at the weekends and Hansaben split her time between cooking and playing the role of family agony aunt.

Jamnadasbhai was a dear man who used to work as an accountant for the Madhvani family at their big sugar estate in Kakira, Uganda. His first job in the UK was working for Alan – now Lord – Sugar at Amstrad. Like many Jewish firms, Amstrad had spotted that the British Indians were hard workers, good employees and represented cheap labour. Jamnadasbhai was one of Alan's first employees and used to take him apples for lunch, because Alan would always be working so hard he'd forget to eat. Jamnadasbhai was always full of praise for 'Mr Sugar' and, many years later when Sandhya and Lord Sugar met in the House of Lords, they shared many stories about my father-in-law.

Sandhya was introduced to me by a family acquaintance of ours called Ramesh Mashru. He was her cousin. She and I met a couple of times in the usual semi-arranged Gujarati way. It began in February 1980 with my parents calling me into their room and sternly informing me that it was time I settled down (I would be twenty-seven in the June). My mother knew Ramesh's mother – and a couple of days later he called to say that he would pick me up on Friday along with his cousin, Sandhya, who worked as a personnel officer at Glaxo on Green Street in London.

I was very taken with Sandhya. Compared to me – very streets-of-Harrow – Sandhya seemed very West End and sophisticated. And my family was very old-fashioned compared to her more modern, younger one. But we chatted and agreed, 'Yes, we can do this, we can put a life together.' At Easter that year – on Good Friday, in fact – we got engaged.

In those days, weddings in the Gujarati community were much more like a business merger than a romantic novel. You had to like each other, but it was about finding someone who would complement you and shared your aspirations. That was enough to get engaged; the falling-in-love part came later. (I truly believe that if you don't go looking for love, love will find you.)

Sandhya's uncle Ramesh Sachdev was on holiday when he heard the news of our engagement – he immediately travelled back to London to inspect and interrogate me with many questions, in order to approve the marriage of his niece. He is one of Sandhya's favourite people in the world and, since our engagement, he has been a dear friend to me. There are very few people whose opinions I trust more in the world on family and business matters than Ramesh, and he's been by our side now for forty years. I have a really strong bond with him – we share the spiritual guidance of the same guru (Morari Bapu), we go on holidays together, and our wives get on, which is always a bonus.

Due to my final exams (as I then thought – though the story was to alter) and the pressures of the new business, Sandhya and I spent little time together between engagement and marriage. Because of my mortgage commitments, I couldn't even afford to buy her an engagement ring, though I hope I have made up for it since.

By July of that year, I was married, and I have never regretted it for one second. Sandhya and I are opposites. I am a talker, she is a listener. I am restless, she is calm. I can get a little carried away, while she is practical and down to earth. She also has very high standards: where I would look for compromise, she will simply push until she is satisfied… which makes me wonder why she married me!

Above all, Sandhya is genuine and natural. There is no phoniness about her. She is direct and will tell people what she thinks. Whereas I will always sit on the fence, trying to work out the optimal outcome.

We couldn't really afford a honeymoon either. I am afraid to say that my approach was: 'Why waste money on going away?' But in the end I relented and, courtesy of Freddie Laker, whose airline was the Ryanair of the time, we booked a week in New York on a credit card. Or, more accurately, because I'd maxed out my own credit card, I used Sandhya's to pay for the trip! On the plane, we discussed my family. She said she found it large and competitive, quite boisterous compared to her own which had more propriety, despite being more modern in its outlook.

During the trip we made a visit to Toronto to see Sandhya's aunt, Pravina (Sandhya's mother's younger sister), and her husband Kiran. We are all similar in age and the couple would become close friends. Kiran and I both love golf and we have been on many annual holidays together.

As I got to know Sandhya more, I knew I had made the right choice. She has provided me with unfailing love and support in what I wanted to do. In her middle age, she has rightly turned more to her own interests, running our family charitable trusts and dedicating herself to the work of the Self-Realization Fellowship church in Baker Street.

Now, looking back over a happy marriage, I believe there is a reason that Sandhya and I never met before we did (although our parents were in different social worlds and different parts of London, there was a possibility we could have met back in Uganda). God brought her into my life at just the right time, when I was open to having a partner at my side; even though, like a typical business person, I was always thinking about the next deal. Thankfully, when we did meet, I had enough good sense (and my parents' urgings were part of this) to recognise that she was the woman for me. It has been the best choice I have ever made.

Just before we were married, Sandhya took the momentous decision to give up her job at Glaxo and begin helping to run our sub-post office business in Watford. My brother Pankaj was already helping me run it, but when Sandhya and I got engaged we'd discussed my business plan and she'd agreed to support it. She never told me what she earned at Glaxo or I'm not sure I'd have let her join me! Her large salary and good pension were a much safer bet than my aspirations at that stage.

Following my marriage, Fast Finance continued to grow at a prodigious rate. In the evenings, I would meet finance clients at home (I was living with Sandhya, my parents and my extended family in a house on Claremont Avenue in Kenton); they often couldn't get time off to meet during the day and I preferred to use the house as it was more presentable than the office. So three or four times a week, around 8 p.m., the bell would ring and a meeting would start.

One of my biggest coups was on the night before the final stage of my accountancy exams. I was preparing to head off to Watford the next morning for my final exams. Then there was a knock on the door and I opened it to see four big Pakistani guys, burly fellows in *kurtas* (traditional tunics) and wool jackets. We let them in and they told their story. They'd bought eight shops from the receivers and they wanted it financed within forty-eight hours. One of them said: 'Name your price. If you do it in forty-eight hours, we'll pay you.'

So I had a snap decision to make: either I did a bit more revision and got a good night's sleep before my exam or I tried to make this deal happen for them. I told them it would cost £2,000 – my usual 1 per cent – and they said fine. Well, I worked all night, borrowing a neighbour's typewriter to get the package done. In the morning, I took it to the Stevenage branch of Barclays Bank where I knew one of the managers, Olly Webster. Because it was one of the bigger branches of the bank, I knew Olly had the discretion to approve the proposal. He said yes, and I got an offer letter out the following day to the estate agent. I missed my exam, but the next day one of the Pakistanis turned up with an envelope containing £2,000 in cash. Two grand then was like £30,000 now, so the personal impact of earning that in a single night was massive.

The whole business caused a bit of friction with my father. My brother Pankaj was getting married and I overheard my father and sister talking about the cost of the wedding expenses, which are normally covered by the parents. So I butted in and said, 'Look, I can help, I just earned two grand overnight.'

My father was always very concerned for me. He had the bedroom at the front of the house and watched these strangers coming and going through the big double windows like some sort of gatekeeper. Whenever the phone rang, he'd race over to answer it first. I think the finance business frightened him a little bit and – as he'd tried to do in Uganda – he wanted to protect me. He asked Sandhya about the Pakistanis a few days later, calling her into his room: 'Who were those men who came to the door? What kind of business is Dolar doing exactly?' I think he thought they were gangsters and that I was somehow involved in crime! I swear he was convinced a policeman was about to knock next at the door and cart me off.

To her credit, Sandhya told my father off, saying, 'This is his work now. He arranges money from the banks for people who wouldn't otherwise get it; he puts the package together. You see him typing late. That money they brought is just a fee, one he has earned.'

My father argued a bit more but Sandhya stood up to him, and we never heard any more complaints. It was quite a thing in those days for an Indian woman to stand up to her father-in-law, but times were beginning to change. We didn't realise it at the time, but we were becoming modern British Indians.

As for the Barclays branch in Stevenage, they were very happy, and asked me to send them more business. After that, I saw no point in finishing my accountancy exams. By then, qualified chartered accountants were themselves coming to me for advice on raising money for their clients. They didn't have much idea of business financing in those days. Few people did. Oddly enough, we are in a similar position now, as banks seem unwilling to support small companies – an issue that I would try to address when I started my political career.

My experience back then made me a specialist in business and corporate finance, and my network of contacts grew ever wider. Every year the big banks would put on networking events. Barclays bought tickets for a snooker tournament in Nottingham, NatWest had a cricket event at Lords, and so on. I'd go along, meet the branch managers and find out where they fitted in the hierarchy. A big branch, like the Barclays in Stevenage, would be a grade eight, which meant the manager had a lending discretion of around £200,000. All of this was in my head, so when a client came in needing a certain size of loan, I'd go to an appropriate branch. It was simply a 'horses for courses' strategy. I even got to the point where a lot of the bank managers who'd had to reject someone's application would then refer them on to me.

Fast Finance scaled very quickly. By January 1983, I was no longer involved in the post office, which I gave to my brother Pankaj. I say gave, but the fact is he, Kantesh and I had been working together in various ways, pooling and separating our assets whenever it seemed right to do so, so it was already in part his business. (This way of multiplying wealth and security together is very Gujarati.)

As a result of these changes, Fast Finance relocated to rented offices (£6,000 a year) at 104a High Street, Wealdstone. The move was a real step up. We were on the first floor and shared the building with EMF, a business transfer agency on the second floor, and Mann & Co, a residential mortgage brokers, downstairs.

Gone was the dusty room above the post office. Now we had a reception where my new PA, Kay Mills, and her assistant, Michelle, would sit. Kay was unbelievably good at setting the right tone for the place and always helped to put clients at ease. I could always tell when she thought a client might be difficult when she showed them into my office – complete with its own bar – and her instinct was never wrong.

One such occasion involved raising money for a scaffolding company that was going under. The fortunes of these construction-related businesses tend to go in cycles. You have five good years and one really bad year, and then you get into trouble because you have no cash reserves.

One of the owners of this scaffolding outfit came to see me from his base in West Ham. He was a tough-looking white guy with a shaved head, angry because he was in receivership and probably a few other reasons besides. He almost walked out straight away as soon as he saw the colour of my skin. He was visibly fuming when we were introduced.

I said to him, 'Don't be silly. You are in difficulties. Barclays are coming into your company, appointing receivers. They will take over and sell it. If you want me to help you, I will show you the way, but there's a fee for that.'

He said, 'OK, mate,' but was still very uncertain of me.

I said, 'Can you find a relation of yours with a good credit history?'

We talked it through and agreed his brother-in-law would be suitable. I said that I needed to see his last three sets of accounts, and he said he'd post them to me.

'No,' I interjected, 'you'll go home now, get them and bring them right back to me. If your company was a patient, it would need major surgery and it cannot be delayed.' I'd often use medical terminology because by then many people were used to having Indian doctors and I felt like it gave me a bit more authority.

So the man did, and in the following week he brought his brother-in-law to see me. We sold the business to him, raising the finance for it in a new loan.

The original bankers were happy; they got their money. There was also now a new business, co-owned by the brother-in-law, and it looked very well, with around a £30,000 surplus to ensure long-term cash flow.

A few weeks later, the scaffolder brought round a bottle of Johnnie Walker for me.

He said, 'I wanted to say thank you and also to tell you something.'
'What's that?' I said.

'I've been a member of the National Front all my life. You helping me, doing such a good job, has made me realise how wrong
I was. You didn't just save my business. You saved my marriage,
everything, really.' It was another small victory for integration.

I helped a lot of people like that, and many of the companies
I helped grew, trading out of their problems. A lot of the bank
managers were scared to use their discretion, to go to head office
and make the case, so I helped them, too. It's even worse now,
with credit scoring that doesn't really reflect the fundamentals of a
business, and a kind of herd mentality affecting lenders' decision-
making, especially in times of recession.

Of course, recession is often exactly the time that you *should* lend,
as you are able to secure preferential rates for the lender and a
lower percentage of lending, which is more secure. People seem to
have forgotten that.

My skill was showing how cases that were marginal could be
made viable. I had learned from the Indian community how family
members could help in this process. If there were a situation where
people didn't have any money to put in, to finance or refinance a
business, we'd get them to look at all the properties in the family.
House prices had gone up. So we'd re-mortgage a house and raise
the capital to inject into the business, which would act as surety for
further bank loans. It was common for Indians in those days to put
wider family money into a business.

I soon began to apply the same thinking to clients from other
groups. Even Jewish businesses, which had their own, much
longer-established networks, began to come to me. By 1982 – one

year after not being able to afford an engagement ring – I was making around £60,000 in clear profit, which is over £200,000 in today's money. Partly this was because Sandhya and Pankaj were putting in the hours running the shop. Sandhya was also typing out the proposals for new finance deals after everyone at home had gone to sleep. Their hard work left me free to concentrate on the people side of the finance business.

The finance system I eventually set up was based on the principle of a client having 'skin in the game' to a ratio of 40:60. In other words, if they came up with 40 per cent of the money, the bank would cover the 60 per cent and take charge on the lease, which was effectively unsecured lending.

Sometimes clients didn't understand that it was my connections, reputation and knowledge that were enabling the loan. There was one Englishman who came to see me. He was buying a video shop, which was a new concept in those days. He had been to his own bank – the NatWest in Southend-on-Sea – and his loan request had been declined. He came to see me and I managed to get the finance through the NatWest in Stanmore. Afterwards, the man got in a grump and took this up with the head office: 'I went to see my local bank, they wouldn't do it for me. Here's an Indian guy who did it, charged me a fee, and then the loan came through, from the very same bank!'

He took it very personally, somewhat denigrating me in the process, at least by implication. But the bank just gave an explanation along the lines of: 'The case came from Dolar Popat, and we have been doing business with him for many years. And so far none of his clients have let us down, so we go by his recommendations.'

I soon realised that I couldn't run Fast Finance on my own. I turned to someone who had helped me and my family when I took our first step into business, brokering a deal to help fund the purchase of the sub-post office in Watford. His name was Roy Hawkins. When I approached him, he said he would be happy to join me; so was an Irishman called Tom Fahey. Together, we advised and helped finance large numbers of small and medium-sized businesses. We became the go-to people for smaller-scale corporate finance, with a large number of contacts with many different banks, including Barclays, Barclays Mercantile, NatWest and the Royal Bank of Scotland.

I needed Roy and Tom not just because of their business acumen but also because – even though Britain was beginning to diversify culturally during the 1980s – many people were still uncomfortable dealing with an Indian. By contrast, Roy and Tom were always happy to help people irrespective of their ethnic background (and Roy continues working with my family to this day).

One of the ideas we developed together was following up on people and businesses we had helped get finance, ensuring everything was running smoothly. All too often people pay only lip service to the idea of 'after sales service', but we meant it and did the work. I am still in touch now with some of the business owners that I first met over thirty years ago, like the owners of the Bestway Cash and Carry Group, which now has a turnover of around £3 billion.

Although Fast Finance was growing under our joint stewardship, it became apparent to me that I needed to develop another type of business. As it turned out, it would be a care home business; at first, this wasn't for profit but for family reasons.

In January 1983, as I moved Fast Finance out of the flat above the post office in Watford to the premises in Wealdstone, my first son Rupeen was born. (Oddly enough a change in commercial or domestic property has coincided with the birth of each of my three sons: with Rupeen we got the new Fast Finance office; with Paavan we got Clavering Nursing Home; and with Shivaan we got The Knoll, our house in Stanmore. I believe the births brought me good luck.)

It was a very exciting moment, Rupeen being born. But for Sandhya, the first few months of motherhood were very challenging. Having been a professional working for a multinational and then someone who worked all hours for a family business, she was now suddenly stuck at home.

To make matters worse, we'd moved out of the family home in Kenton a couple of months after Rupeen's birth, meaning Sandhya was even more isolated. I don't think either of us realised at the time how much we'd need help raising a child. She developed post-natal depression. It's nothing to be ashamed of – many women suffer this unfortunate condition, especially when they are married to hard-working businessmen who are often home late and whose minds are consumed with their projects. I felt incredibly guilty. I was so preoccupied with my work that I didn't spot what was happening straight away, and when I did I didn't really understand it.

It got quite bad. I knew I had to act, so I bought Clavering Residential Home in Harrow for Sandhya to run. It meant that she had something to keep her occupied, something that had more substance and prospects than the post office. But it also meant that we had the excuse we needed to hire an au pair. At the time, there was no custom within the British Indian community for hiring someone to help with the children and my parents really wouldn't have approved of it. But, with our Clavering commitments, we now had a good enough reason. We immediately set about making some changes, converting the nineteen-bed home into a 22-bed one.

But I need to backtrack, I think, to show how a business focused on financial services and advice morphed into one that almost exclusively provided care for the elderly. Part of the reason was that Fast Finance suddenly had lots of competition. Almost overnight, it seemed, we had gone from being the only finance brokerage in the UK specialising in small to medium-sized businesses to one that had to fight to keep its dominant position.

This was an important discovery for me: that as soon as any business idea is matured and proven, up springs the competition. In many ways it was my own fault. I'd talk about what I was doing: some of my biggest competitors were east African Indians whose families I had financed!

But it's a good thing, competition – it's what capitalism is all about. Competition helps to raise standards and lower prices – it's just rather turbulent if you are caught in the middle of all the action.

For all that, it was a request for advice at Fast Finance that took us into care homes. I hadn't really heard of care homes or residential homes as a business, but one day a consultant psychiatrist of Sri Lankan extraction rang me asking for help in raising money. I went to see him in Croydon, mistakenly thinking he had said 'restaurant' as the place of appointment, rather than 'rest home'! I was expecting we were to have a meal.

Anyway, my mistake became instantly clear as he showed me round the place he wanted to recapitalise, which was called Birdhurst Nursing Home. I suddenly became aware of this whole new area of business of care homes and rest homes for the elderly. I was struck by how quickly a bank manager was willing to lend to Bird-hurst and I looked into the viability of the sector. I saw at once that it produced steady long-term revenues and was completely different to Fast Finance, which was essentially a transactional business.

The purchase of Clavering itself is quite a story. It was worth £350,000, but the owner wanted £450,000. We said we'd pay it. And then he changed his mind, and said he wanted £480,000. We said we'd pay it. Then he wanted another ten grand, so we gave another ten grand. I just wanted it, because my wife was unhappy and I loved her. To give an idea of the figures involved in today's terms, the site that we paid £490,000 for in June 1984 is worth around £6 million now. By then I had such a good reputation in the banking sector that I had no problem raising the money. (We still have Clavering as a matter of fact, and in November 2018 we received planning permission to rebuild it into a new 78-bed care home.)

So, buying Clavering was another important decision made and one that I intimately link to Sandhya, who got the whole thing off the ground. Little did either of us know, this deal would be the foundation of a whole other business enterprise separate from Fast Finance. I like to think of Clavering as the first step in the creation of a two-act career. (Or perhaps there have been three acts – I was also making my first steps in politics at this time, which I shall cover in due course.)

I have to say, and not just as an afterthought, that Sandhya was brilliant at running the pastoral side of Clavering, which is an important aspect of a nursing home. She was overseeing the general manager, dealing with residents and relations, banking, invoicing and doing the cash and carry runs. It was full on and it really brought out two of her strongest characteristics: how caring she is and her demand for high standards. It took a toll on her health, though, and she developed asthma as a consequence of the pressure.

All of our clients at Clavering were English and a good many of the employees were from the Caribbean, at least at that stage. I remember once an English woman saying to my wife, 'I don't want that black nurse to look after me.' But Sandhya subtly educated this lady, so that after a while the patient realised that this nurse was the best at looking after her.

In our work at Clavering, I suppose we were in a way at the forefront of the growing culture of diversity that has been a characteristic of Britain since I moved here. In my opinion, an important part of making a multicultural society work is the realisation that it is not all about the relationship between immigrants and the indigenous population. It's also about consolidating relationships between immigrant groups of different eras and origins; we all have a lot to learn from each other about how to be British, each in our own ways. In turn, the indigenous population begins to see its own identity in a more fluid way.

The basic fact is, most indigenous Brits are now welcoming to immigrants; it's only a relatively small percentage who are not. With time, with more dialogue, more understanding, that small percentage will shrink even further. But these divisions in attitude are also a reflection of the incoming immigrant numbers year on year, which is why it has become such a big policy issue in recent years.

It's not been easy balancing an Indian and British identity at the same time, not to mention a residual African one. I think of this when I look at a photograph taken by Sandhya when Rupeen was a year old in 1984. There is my father in a blue suit and white shirt, top button done up, looking fairly grizzled; my mother in her sari, beaming away at her grandson; me in a cream safari suit sitting between them, with Rupeen on my knee; and Sandhya, in fashionable modern Western clothes. So there we all are, a family defined by three different worlds: India, Uganda and Britain. And for me, both before that photo was taken and since, there has been an added professional dimension to this issue of identity. I have always had two careers in everything I have done: studying accountancy while working at Wimpy; managing a finance business while investigating the other business of care homes; managing care homes while exploring politics in the evenings. Even now, I'm a trade envoy while being a whip.

The year 1984 was an important one for another reason. It was then that I first met my guru, Morari Bapu, at a religious recital organised by the Madhvani family. Though it would be at least another decade before I fully became one of Bapu's devotees (I'd meet him again in 1994 and 1998, and regularly thereafter), I was struck even then by how liberal he was for a Hindu, as his talk was more about the spiritual side than the religious. I found his approach very modern; he had a Western outlook and was very practical. His explanations of sacred texts were simpler and felt more relevant than other people's. Bapu had a family (in contrast to the many spiritual leaders who remain single) and I liked his use of music and humour to accompany his messages – this helped him attract a new generation of British-born Indians to his nine-day recitals.

As I mentioned earlier, Bapu teaches three main qualities: truth, love and compassion (*satya*, *prem* and *karuna*). These are the founding qualities that build bridges between different religions and communities, but also a firm base on which to conduct one's personal life.

6

FACING CHALLENGES

Fast Finance continued to grow, and represented bigger and bigger clients. Some of the people I raised money for in the 1980s are on the *Sunday Times* Rich List now. It's interesting when I meet them at functions: some remember me, some don't (or affect not to). Of course, the smaller fish always remember you – but that's the way of the world.

In September 1988, Sandhya and I moved into The Knoll in Stanmore (as I've mentioned, the house where we still live today). We'd pass the house every day on the way to nursery with Rupeen and one morning Sandhya spotted a 'for sale' sign in the driveway. We'd already bought another house on Royston Grove – a few minutes' walk from Clavering – and were planning on moving in a few weeks, but this house was perfect; it had won an architectural award and was in a fantastic neighbourhood. We desperately wanted it.

I rang the estate agent and he sent over the details. The big problem was that the house was in a very Jewish area – the agents were only advertising the property in the *Jewish Chronicle* – and we weren't convinced they'd sell to an Indian family. I asked Roy, one of my company directors, to go and see it, and once he'd given his OK, phoned the agent.

I got the agent to agree to propose the following to the sellers: that we'd pay the asking price if they agreed to exchange within forty-eight hours and, after that, complete within three months. This would give me enough time to sort a mortgage and our commitments with Royston Grove. They agreed, everything went smoothly and we got to move in to The Knoll later that year.

Some of the Jewish neighbours did not take kindly to the presence of Asians. One family – whom I recall owned a tailoring business – moved out immediately, and their replacements were even worse! But it's important to say that we also made strong friends among the Jewish community, in particular Sabah and Terry Kattan, whose son David became friends with our second son, Paavan; our two families developed a rota system to drop the children at school.

Our new, unfriendly, neighbours were incredulous, even challenging the Kattans one day on why they were 'helping' us. It was a shame, given all our communities have in common, but it brought to light a certain snobbery in parts of the Jewish community that is now much reduced, I am glad to say. We tried and I think succeeded in integrating, and in fact like many Gujaratis learned a lot from our contact with Jews, so many of whose values we share, as I have stressed. The Mezuzah that hung on the frame of our front door as we entered the house for the first time in 1988 is still proudly fixed in the same position today.

In the mid-1980s our family also grew larger, Sandhya blessing me with two other sons besides Rupeen: Paavan, born in 1985, and Shivaan, born in 1988. Between them these three are the beating heart of our family life, and are also now involved in many of our enterprises. But many of those businesses came close to failing when my sons were just boys.

Within a few years, Fast Finance bought a big office building in Harrow, which we named Finance House. As I've mentioned in relation to domestic property, Indians aren't generally big fans of renting; we prefer to have the freehold as an asset, and Finance House offered us that. We had our own offices there, which meant we were now close to a lot of our clients, and Clavering was also nearby. We sold the lease of the property's ground floor to a firm of lawyers and also rented office space to a firm of chartered survey-ors – so we had effectively got ourselves both an in-house legal and surveying team. The building became, somewhat accidentally, like a miniature version of the relationships that have made the City of London so successful: complementary firms working side by side, allowing business to be conducted at speed.

But it was a mistake, this purchase; the timing was wrong. In 1991, the recession hit and property prices crashed. Suddenly, having been making large profits, I was more or less nearly bank-rupt. For the first time in my career I had huge fixed overheads and no income coming in.

I wasn't alone in my predicament. Almost all the banks had stopped lending and many leveraged businesses were in trouble. To make matters worse, interest rates had gone up, which meant my mortgage payments had done the same, creating more financial pain. The banks were also on the hunt to collect as much as they could of their liabilities in order to recapitalise their balance sheet.

We saw similar moments in the 2008 financial crisis. My first rule in business nowadays is: always keep 10 per cent of total bor-rowing in liquidity within the business. I have already explained how Anthony Barber, as Chancellor in the early 1970s, introduced a minimum reserve ratio of 12.5 per cent so banks always kept a portion of unallocated cash on their balance sheets. I just adapted that rule. I think my applying that rule to myself is the only reason Fast Finance survived in this period. Liquidity ratios are something I am completely paranoid about to this day: they are pretty much the first thing I check when I look at company accounts. Setting a liquidity minimum for company borrowing is an act of self-regulation and, in my opinion, doing so is the mark of a responsible company – I'd advise anyone in business to apply a rule of this kind.

Back then, in the dark days of the recession of the late '80s, I knew I had to take steps to resolve problems in the business, and fairly quickly. First, we tried to sell The Knoll, which we had bought for £650,000, but things were so bad we couldn't even get a buyer for much over £400,000; in fact, we couldn't even get a tenant to rent the house at a rate that would cover the mortgage.

This was very stressful. It wasn't just a question of the risk of going broke and the impact that would have on our growing family, it was a question of losing my reputation in the community as a 'master of raising finance'.

However, there *was* a solution, as it turned out. I sat down with Sandhya and we made plans to turn Clavering into a profitable business, using my forensic accounting skills to go through the budget line by line. We also planned to expand in the care home sector, which apart from finance was the commercial area I now knew best. I'd advise any young entrepreneur to diversify like this, so you are never in the position of relying on a single income stream. Two, maybe three, businesses can cover each other's back, if there's a recession. My brothers Pankaj and Kantesh have both used this approach successfully, running a number of businesses simultaneously.

But back at my point of crisis, I needed to act. Extending my credit to its final limit, in March 1992 I bought two care homes in Barnsley from a company called Rockley Dene, which owned a residential home and a nursing home in adjacent properties. The two men who owned Rockley Dene were in financial difficulty themselves. This is how my first deliberate move into the care business began.

I went to see the owners of Rockley Dene to see if I could help with refinancing. I also met the NatWest manager who was running their loan and said he was about to pull the plug. At that stage, I was acting as a commercial loans consultant for NatWest.

So I said to the owners, 'Well, best thing is you sell it.'

They replied, 'We can't find a buyer now.'

I said, 'I'll buy it.'

I actually gave them the asking price. My view was, forget the price, it's generating an amount of income, and I needed that liquid cash to pay for my business and personal overheads. So this is another good tip: when thinking about acquiring a business, look at the cash flow as much as the price.

As I say, there were few banks lending money at this time, but the Bank of Ireland was really new in England and had an appetite to lend. Because I already had a good connection with them (they'd recently opened a branch in Harrow), they agreed to lend for these two homes. It helped that I had Clavering and knew the care home business – no bank would have lent me money if I'd been looking to finance an entirely new venture. At the same time as the deal was going through, Rockley Dene was also struggling to finance a third care home, which had been left half-built. As a rider on our deal, I helped them refinance the project, allowing them to complete the property.

In many ways, this was quite a risky thing to do – taking on a significant liability at a time when the economy seemed to be contracting – but it was the right decision. In fact, I have not looked back since.

However, all this was reliant on having made Clavering profitable. Through making cost savings and finding new clients, Sandhya and I had transformed Clavering from breaking point to making around £70,000 annual profit before we crystallised the Rockley Dene deal. So it was the strength of Clavering and our experience in that business that helped me to raise the finance to expand. It also made it easier for the underwriters to say, 'Hold on, this guy knows the business; he's been in it. He already has one. He's just expanding to buy two more.'

I paid £1.35 million for the Rockley Dene homes, but with expenses on top the total cost worked out at about £1.4 million. I put in £300,000 of my own money, and I borrowed £1.1 million from the bank. My brother Kantesh also put in £150,000 of his money, and I insisted he come in as a 50–50 partner.

So here we see again a principle of immigrant culture in action: families working together to prosper (something that happens far less in indigenous British families). Not everyone has to be involved; by this stage my other brother Manoj, who had been my host when I first came to Britain, had since qualified as an accountant in Canada. He was already on to the next stage of integration into an adoptive society, which is professionalisation (becoming a doctor, lawyer or accountant, mostly). This is usually only achieved in the second or (depending on the country of origin) third generation, but Manoj was always very smart – he was way ahead of the rest of us other Popats in academic terms.

Anyway, back to Rockley Dene. It was a calculated risk. Pretty much double or quits, if one was a poker player (which I am not). The deal could have ended in disaster, with foreclosure on all the properties I was now supporting, and the bankruptcy of three businesses – but it worked out. What I would say to young immigrant entrepreneurs is: do your sums, and if they work out, take the risk. But the hard thing is, sometimes you don't quite know. There is an uncertainty factor, which one could probably compute at between 15 and 30 per cent. It's this part – going for it despite the element of the unknown – which the entrepreneur is being rewarded for if all goes well. That's what socialists forget when they complain about high personal returns on investment.

A lot of business is luck plus hard work. I just happen to have been luckier than most, something my family often remind me of. They laugh about the time I bought a single ticket for a raffle in Canada and ended up winning a car. My career has more often than not been about being in the right place at the right time rather than a progression planned with foresight; I'd say even my peerage had a large slice of luck about it. Like many entrepreneurs, I'm good at seeing an opportunity for a business, but for all the pieces to fall into place is rare. There's a huge element of chance that I've benefited from. Dealing with the recession in 1991 was incredibly painful. It was three years of constant concerns over income and expenditure, but once it was over I felt like I'd taken the only path available to me.

Luckily for me, the risk paid off. Many others went to the wall during this recession, caught in a trap between a sudden halt in demand and rising interest rates. My salvation was that I saw the benefits of diversification straight away. I honestly believe that this

95

was because of my family's experience in Uganda. I had seen – as had my father – how circumstances can suddenly change.

You are in a new paradigm; the old dispensations no longer apply. So what do you do? You act. You act as fast as you possibly can, because as soon as the new information hits your consciousness, it is almost too late. You are in a market, after all, and every day the speed at which information travels in a market is increasing. What is happening in your consciousness is a reflection of a larger phenomenon. Immigrants are often good at acting fast, especially if they have come out of trying circumstances, so maybe there is a small advantage there.

As well as facing financial challenges, I also had to deal with actually managing Rockley Dene. I would travel up to Barnsley once a week to inspect the homes. It was a very different town to London. The people were very friendly but there was a strong Arthur Scargill influence there. I was nervous about how a British Indian businessman from a finance-sector background would go down. On my first visit I met Ann, the matron of the home, and asked her if we could discuss strategy. Another person was lurking in the room, but we weren't properly introduced.

'Strategy?' Ann said in her blunt Yorkshire way. 'I'm a nurse, what do I know about strategy?'

Somewhat warily, I said I wanted to make some changes to the home. Although nurses aren't always commercially minded, their knowledge of how the homes are run is invaluable, and I knew I needed Ann onside if the changes we were planning were going to be successful. So I set out for her how the staff had only had a very small pay increase for the past three years and that we needed to pay more money to the lowest-paid staff. I explained how I also wanted to spruce the place up with some painting and decorating, and to set up a Resident's Association so that I'd be able to hear directly from the residents every week on any issues they felt needed addressing.

Ann was won over, and proved to be a huge asset over the next few years. But, what I hadn't known was that the other person sitting in her office was a government inspector, who spoke glowingly about the new leadership of the home in her report and how the new owner had 'transformed the business'. At a time when it felt like everything was going against me, that was a lucky break.

But if I am making all of this sound like a piece of cake, then that's the wrong impression to give you. It wasn't easy. No sooner had I bought the Rockley Dene homes than Sandhya contracted acute pancreatitis. She was in hospital for four months. So that was a difficult time for both of us. I was a father and a mother to my three children, taking them to school and dropping them back, and at the same time managing to run the Rockley Dene homes, Fast Finance and Clavering. I was so stretched that Ignatius and Roma got on a plane to come and see Sandhya. My family members and our Jewish friend, Terry Kattan, were also very helpful during this difficult period.

It was one of the worst times of my life, actually. More significant than anything had been the death of my brother Suresh in October 1990 from diabetes. He was thirty-two. Suresh was a marvellous brother. His time working in a bookmakers in the UK meant he'd been renamed 'Bob' (Popat was too exotic for his colleagues so he'd become 'Robert', which was soon shortened). I was fond of him and so were my three little boys. He used to take them out on a regular basis, often for a ride on the London Underground, which the boys loved. He left behind his wife, Bhavna, but no children of his own.

The pain of Suresh's passing had a devastating impact on my father. No parent ever wants to outlive their child, and my father's health markedly declined. The man who'd taught me about leadership and who trained me in so many aspects of life – including how to care for my family – passed away himself on 15 October 1991. A lifetime of smoking and stress, added to Suresh's premature death, was too much for him. It's amazing how many Gujarati families suffer when they lose the head of a household. They're often unprepared for who needs to step up, make decisions and support the others. But my father had been prepared; he'd spent years getting me ready. I was so grateful for everything he taught me, and that he was no longer suffering.

The rest of the family all felt the same. They were doing OK, though. My brother Pankaj, for instance, was still at the post office but had also purchased a care home. My dear mother was still alive and living with Pankaj; she would pass away four years later.

Going through these traumas, Sandhya and I struggled on in the business, soon seeing that there was potential to extend Clavering by buying a house next door, rebuilding and extending the home to a property with forty-nine beds. I was helped in that the government was closing down long-stay hospitals across the NHS and tendering for private operators.

This was part of a long-term trend. The introduction of the Community Care Act in 1990 caused health and local authorities to seek alternative ways of providing care for elderly people. Previously, this had primarily been an in-house service, meaning either lots of health visitors to private care homes or stints in long-stay hospitals. The government was keen to close this sort of hospital, which was very expensive to run, and were looking for smaller units in which elderly and often mentally infirm patients could be provided with care in the community. A competition to win care contracts was begun, with fifty-odd companies nationwide being given the opportunity to bid.

I managed to get a ten-year contract for forty-six out of forty-nine beds at Clavering. This was part of Brent and Harrow Health Authority's re-provisioning of the care programme at Shenley Hospital, a long-stay psychiatric institution which was being closed down. Shenley was a vast and terrible place, and with nearly 500 patients, incredibly expensive to run. Some of the horror stories about how patients ended up in there still send a chill down my spine.

We were able to convince the local health authority on the basis of our past performance at Clavering and our experiences at Rockley Dene. On the strength of that decision in principle, we closed the existing Clavering site and commenced a rapid and wide-ranging programme of renovation and additional development to create our projected 49-bed home.

The fixed-term contract helped a lot, obviously, but I still needed to get all the building work done by the opening date. Everything had to be done within budget and on spec so we would be ready to take the Shenley patients as promised.

Then came another crisis. A few months before my NHS-contracted deadline for opening, my builder went bust, owing me and others a fair bit of cash. Disaster.

So without any knowledge in the building trade, I suddenly had to find people – electricians and plumbers, and so on – to complete the building work. None of the subcontractors employed by this now-bankrupt builder would work for me. The electrician and the plasterer and the outfitters were all saying no, because the job was associated with a non-payer. So I went to the electrical supplies shop which was also owed money by my builder. I told him my story and said, 'Look, I'll pay every penny owed, if you put me in touch with the electrician.' I gave the shop and the electrician some cash in advance and then one by one the other subcontractors came back onto the job. The refurbishment of Clavering cost me over £100,000 more than it should have done, but the important thing was to open the home on time and to start fulfilling the contract. So this is another tip: take the long-term view, even if it costs you a bit more in the short term.

An added bonus of having to orchestrate getting Clavering finished was that I learned a lot about the building trade. This meant I gained the confidence I needed in the future to either build care homes from scratch or to renovate other properties.

With both Clavering and the two Rockley Dene homes in ownership, I was almost by accident becoming pretty close to being an expert in the care home business, which grew prodigiously as a sector during the 1990s. It's not the same as being an expert in care itself, which involves medical and nursing professionalism, but there is a separate business side to all this, and that is what I learned – moving fast and thinking on my feet as usual, which I seem to have been doing ever since I left Uganda. In fact, sitting down to write this book sometimes seems like the first time I have drawn breath in the intervening forty-eight years!

Looking back, it's easy to see why I was so drawn to the care industry. It had all the elements I used to get as a waiter in Wimpy: a people-centric business where there's lots of interaction. You're constantly dealing with relatives and residents, often from the English community, so you feel like you're part of the mainstream. And with a care home, you know you're undertaking a big responsibility: the old and the ill need proper support, and families often simply aren't able to give it. We helped the residents, but the biggest impact was usually on helping their families get back to a normal life.

I sold the two care homes in Barnsley in 1996 but retained the company registration of Rockley Dene Homes Ltd and used it to acquire a site situated at 175–185 Cricklewood Lane, Barnet. Planning permission for a 93-bed nursing home was obtained, and on the strength of our ability to provide care, as shown at Clavering, I was able to negotiate a further contract with Brent and Harrow Health Authority, for two blocks of thirty-two beds. This made it financially viable for us to proceed with the development of what ultimately became Candle Court Nursing Home, which opened in August 1996.

Utilising the proceeds of the original Barnsley homes, we were also able to purchase a site in Cambridge, one that already had the benefit of planning permission for a forty-bed nursing home. We commenced development of this and it opened in June 1997 under the name Cherry Hinton Care Home, which we matured to profitability within two years.

These were years of very hard work and lots of stress. I found myself needing spiritual guidance and, remembering our previous meetings, I went to meet Bapu during a trip to India in 1998 and asked him if I could host a recital in London. The event took place the following year, as I will describe in a later chapter; I mention it here because this was a period in which my business life and spiritual leanings were beginning to weave together.

In 1999, I set up a holding company called Elite Care Holdings, which in time became my core business. It became the TLC Group in 2007, with the letters in the company's new name standing for 'Truth, Love and Compassion'– an idea suggested by my son Paavan in light of Bapu's watchwords. I wanted these three words to both act as a beacon and as a statement of commitment in the work I was doing in our present homes and on future developments. I think ours was probably the first care home company in Britain to brand its business in this way.

TLC was very successful. As the company grew, so did the number of staff, ranging from cleaners and handymen to managers and accountants; at its maximum it employed around 400 people. I was very involved with everyone, treating staff more or less as family members. This is a very Gujarati approach, but it works well in all small and medium-sized businesses. It's less successful when companies become very large.

A key person in the office was Kay Mills, who had joined me as a PA at Fast Finance when the company had its first proper office in Wealdstone. Incredibly polished and diplomatic, Kay was my right-hand woman at TLC, acting as my corporate voice on many occasions and meeting important clients on my behalf – but equally happy to babysit the kids.

As the company grew, we had to professionalise. That meant bringing people like Duncan Rogers on board as Operations Director; he had a background in the building industry. Another key figure was John O'Kane, who started out as a long-haired and dishevelled handyman (I know he won't mind me saying that!). But I soon saw that there was something about John. He had very good attention to detail and a tremendous loyalty to the company and our family. All he needed was an opportunity, and he worked his way up from doing odd repair and maintenance jobs to becoming a health and safety officer, and now he is a senior manager. This wasn't my doing; John developed himself, but it has been a pleasure to watch his progress.

Manish Chotai was another such individual who was a qualified chartered accountant working as a manager at H. W. Fisher. He became TLC's financial controller, alongside setting up his own accountancy practice, Chotai & Co.

As more and more people went into the care home business (partly my own fault, as I encouraged friends and relatives to follow in my footsteps) and it became increasingly regulated, it was more difficult for TLC to maintain profits. I began looking around again for opportunities to diversify, an instinct that was crystallised by the heavy legislation brought in under the Care Standards Act of 2000. It wasn't that we weren't providing high standards of care – we were, and we were also well able to abide by the new provisions – but that projecting revenue streams from new investments now seemed much more difficult. So we halted future developments of care home businesses until the effects and implications of the Care Standards Act became known.

The care industry went through a real boom following the government's launch of the 'care in the community' concept. Entrepreneurs like me were drawn to it as it combined the opportunity to work in a people-centric business – meaning high job satisfaction – with solid returns. But the shift in legislative approach since 2000 has frightened private sector providers, reducing both their freedom and their returns. Now we have an ageing population yet fewer care homes, a shortage of nurses and a poorly paid profession.

The profile of residents has changed as they're now older and less mobile – which makes them harder to look after – and in some communities (including the British Indian community) there remains a real stigma about putting family members into care. These elements are now coming together to create a perfect storm that will leave millions of people in incredibly difficult circumstances.

There is another lesson for the entrepreneur here. Sometimes legislation can seem like your friend, as with the Community Care Act of 1990, and sometimes it can seem like your enemy, as with the Care Standards Act of 2000. There was nothing wrong with that second act in principle, it just wasn't friendly to entrepreneurs. What the government is doing is balancing the needs of society and business. That is of course right. There must be high standards of care, and obviously there must be some regulation. But, as an entrepreneur, you need to balance the benefits of legislated regulation against the possible risks it can bring to your business case.

As a new century began, the bottom line was that I needed to diversify again. The hotel business seemed an obvious route to go down. To put it crudely, the business model of 'bodies in beds' is very similar to 'heads on pillows'. Developments require the same room size and the same building costs, and provide pretty much the same returns. The only major difference is that hotels are less regulated and 'run' by the central reservations system. I proceeded in the belief that TLC Group's future was best suited to investing in a similar business (i.e. switching our expertise from building and operating care homes to building and operating budget hotels).

I did my research. In the UK at the time, we had a very small budget hotel market; less than 10 per cent of what was available in France and America. It seemed to me like a market for the future. So

I bought a pub that was closing down as a result of anti-monopoly legislation (breweries no longer being allowed to have too many pubs tied to their products). The site, which was in Stratford in East London, had a big car park, which fitted in with my plans.

As part of this plan, I successfully approached the Holiday Inn chain as a potential franchisee. I had stayed at Express by Holiday Inns in America and there were not that many in Britain, although there were plenty of larger Holiday Inns. These Express by Holiday Inns or their equivalents would become the norm in many towns, with the growth of Travelodge and Premier Inn, but they weren't when I began. The franchise with Holiday Inn – a brand well known throughout the world – was agreed on a twenty-year term.

With the franchise in the bag, planning permission was not long coming, so what remained was construction, and after the redevelopment of Clavering I had the confidence and knowledge for it. The new hotel was completed both on time and on budget, opening in October 2002.

In terms of location, again my luck was a factor. Stratford was in those days a very deprived part of London. We were the first to build a hotel around there, as we knew there was a local regeneration plan, but we had no idea the Olympics were going to completely transform the entire area.

Other ventures included a site in Shepherd's Bush that was meant to become another budget hotel. However, because of planning issues it became a compromise between hotel and residential, a brand called Staybridge Suites (also by Holiday Inn).

The consequence of this change of overall business strategy was that I decided to sell all of our care homes. As it turned out, the transaction ended up being a bit of a mess because of due diligence issues on the part of the buyer's banks. I had to buy all the homes back a year later! It cost me £1 million, that little quarrel, but it was a question of my reputation again; I was the person registered as being responsible for our residents' care, which was a responsibility I had to take very seriously. And you know what? The buy-back was a nightmare at the time but I am glad it happened. In the years since, I have come to realise that care homes are a more satisfying business than hotels exactly because of what might seem like problems. You are looking after the most vulnerable people. You can talk to them, find out their problems and really help them. I realised that I actually enjoyed this compared to the more automatic aspects of running hotels, even if the latter made more business sense in some respects.

That's why the TLC Group is now focused on care homes again, with two sites in Potters Bar, one in Cricklewood, one in Camberley, one in Barnet, two in Harrow and two in Cambridge.

Our recently built property in Harrow, Karuna Manor, is an award-winning, state-of-the-art care home for people of Hindu extraction. It caters specifically for the vegetarian community, with in-house chefs preparing delicious Gujarati food. Good communication is at the heart of providing great care, so as well as English, Gujarati, Swahili and Hindi are also spoken by staff. In addition to sixty en suite rooms, spacious lounges and dining areas, the home also has unrivalled facilities, including a Hindu temple, a hair and beauty salon, a boutique shop, a water garden and an in-house cinema. There isn't anything else like it in the United Kingdom. It is less my work than that of my son Paavan (to whom I handed over principal management of TLC Group in 2010), but I feel very proud. We have been early movers in something significant: Karuna

Manor is the first home of its kind for the British Indian community and has set a brand standard.

I want to say a little more about what Karuna Manor represents, as it is important to me personally. As a community, we British Indians have spent the past fifty years trying to better ourselves – first by getting a good job, then by buying a house and car to secure a better future for our families, and then, in later years, securing the best education for our children. Throughout this process, we've integrated successfully into British society, and, as I have stressed, integration is the key to the success of our community. But we are now at a crossroads: we have inspired the new generation of British-born Indians to be the very best they can be; we now have a moral duty to provide for the elderly members of our community who got us here. It is disappointing that it has taken the British Indian community so long to come forward. In that way I admire the Jewish and Muslim communities for what they do for their members.

The role of community leaders is to take their community forward in new directions, hoping they are the right ones. This is how I would define community leadership, and it is why I have been keen to address this issue of an ageing population: to embrace it as an historic opportunity to take the British Indian community to the next level in terms of how it cares for itself.

People in the British Indian community are living longer than ever before – as is true of the British population in general – and this is a major achievement of modern science and healthcare. While an ageing population provides tremendous opportunities for our community, it also presents many challenges, and ones that many members of our community are concerned that we are inadequately prepared for. We are effectively sitting on a time bomb.

I have been an advisor for Nightingale Hammerson (an independent charity that has been serving the Jewish community for over 170 years). The Jewish community is ageing much faster than the British Indian population, but they are far better prepared: its population is around 250,000, but they have thirteen specialist care homes. This is not only because the Jewish community settled in Britain earlier than British Indians, but also because it is an issue to which they have given collective thought – something British Indians are only beginning to do now.

The biggest concern for ageing, particularly in the British Indian community, is loneliness. No one to speak to; nowhere to go. Loneliness helps usher in depression, dementia and other illnesses. A recent study by the University of California has found that feeling lonely almost doubles the risk of an elderly person dying.

Nobody wants to talk about this. You can talk about politics and religion, but if you mention loneliness you empty the room. Many people misunderstand these challenges and turn to the government and the NHS for solutions. The NHS has had great success in extending life, but so much so that it is now a victim of its own achievements.

As a Conservative, I have always believed that the role of the state is limited. With budget pressures and an ageing population, that is true now more than ever.

I feel that, as a community, we need to look more positively at ageing, to develop new ideas under the banner of what's now being described as 'productive ageing'. This does not mean that everybody has to be in the workplace, but that we must look seriously at what older people bring to society.

In countries like India there is still no concept of retirement and people continue working until they die, often simply because there are so many people dependent on their career for their livelihood. Sons and daughters do take over this role to an extent, but the need to share income often devolves back to the head of the family.

So, there is still a long way to go, but at least we are on our way. I am lucky in that my wife's views are very much in line with my own on this. Sandhya is currently working with the Lohana Community Ladies Group to create a support 'hotline' for elderly women who are lonely.

We must avoid seeing all this as the government's problem. We should focus on trying to prevent as much illness as possible happening in the first place by promoting self-help and better medical awareness among the elderly. And, as I have always said, we need more community centres (like the recently established Jasper Centre, a centre in Harrow that focuses on elderly members of the British Indian community) than we do more *mandirs*, as we Hindus call our temples.

Older people can make a valuable contribution and we should be adapting to find ways to include them in the workplace, utilising their skills in a way that makes them happy and keeps them involved in society. So we must do more to address the fear of technology within the elderly sectors of our community. We must educate older people and encourage them to use the internet, email, mobile technology and services like WhatsApp for their own benefit, as well as help them track their own health through the latest medical gadgets.

As I get older myself and look back over my business career, I feel quite proud of what I was able to make of my life given that I left school with no formal education. My success as a self-employed businessperson has not only helped me raise my living standards but also helped me avoid the prejudice that I would have no doubt encountered more often if I had always worked for others. As I think I have shown, there was risk all along, but what I have found is that the best way to minimise the risk is to do your research before committing yourself. Of course, you have to work very hard, too – a lot of would-be young entrepreneurs today don't seem to realise that!

What today's young businesspeople need is a good dose of recession. Having been through two, I have come to the conclusion that recession is a good thing for business. It forces a company to clean up its act. Recessions mature you, obliging you to ignore the extraneous and focus on fundamentals: cost cutting; careful management; and good communication with your customers and staff.

For some businesspeople, recession also provides the best opportunity to make money: buying at the bottom so they can sell at the top. Others just have to batten down the hatches and wait for the good times to come again, hoping against hope that they have the sense to continue applying the lessons of austerity when they come, but that they also have the appetite to risk funds in an investment when an opportunity (or a necessity) presents itself.

It is strange how the word 'austerity' has lost all its sense of virtue in Britain, being associated only with pain. We British Indians know its virtuous qualities well, with our yogic traditions of fasting and abnegation of the self. I do wonder whether Britain shall live to rue the apparent abandonment of austerity in the current political phase. At any rate, the crazy spending plans currently proposed by the Labour Party make no sense at all to me, either as a businessman or as a politician.

7

GETTING INVOLVED

I remember my fellow Tory and east African exile Shantoo Ru-parell once saying, 'Unless we participate politically, our interests will be in grave danger – we must participate politically to avoid a repeat of what happened to Asians in Uganda, Kenya, Tanzania and other countries.' It was certainly the case that Asians in many countries besides Uganda had been subject to exclusion and discrimination, if not outright exile.

What Shantoo said remains true: ethnic minorities must be constantly vigilant about the dangers of avoiding civic responsibility. One of the first times the British Indian community saw the effects of this was the introduction of legislation permitting Sunday trading in 1994. This really hit the Indian shopkeeper who had been accustomed to have their premises open all hours, benefitting from the fact that larger stores remained closed.

The Sunday Trading Act was, if I am not mistaken, the first piece of legislation to directly affect Ugandan Asians following our arrival from Africa; there was no representation of our interests at either national or local level. Even British Indians themselves did not seem to grasp the implications. I went to the Neasden Temple to rally support and explain the consequences of the new act, but my words fell on deaf ears.

Even now, there are many ethnic minorities that do not seem to understand that if you wish to control your destiny within a society, you need to get involved. To me, some of those with immigrant heritage in Britain seem, on the contrary, to be more interested in promoting their sense of being an outsider – as if it is, simultaneously and rather perversely, something worthy of both celebration and lament.

The connections between culture, community, ethnicity and national affiliation are complex and provoke equally complex philosophical questions. There are sociological factors (real situations, patent distortions and wickedly persistent problems) that continue to make successive members of immigrant communities feel like they don't and can't belong in Britain. However, the blame for the existence of some of these barriers lies not with the state, nor with general British society, but with immigrant communities themselves.

I've long held an appreciation for the importance of civic duty and the importance of the political system, but I never expected politics to become such a central part of my life. Alongside my business career, my political activism grew organically, starting locally in the Asian areas of Harrow and Barnet, and with a grass-roots sense of duty to my community and country.

I joined the Conservative Party in January 1980, following the election of Margaret Thatcher the previous May. I was enthused by her and exercised by the nationalisation policies of the Labour Party. By then I had already been engaged in grass-roots activity, going to local party meetings and other political gatherings. The specific factors that made me join the Conservatives were: industrial strikes; the three-day week of winter 1974; nationalised companies including British Airways making huge losses; and the socialist policies of Harold Wilson in the mid-1970s. The Winter of Discontent (1978–79) and the perceived decline of Britain's manufacturing sector were also big drivers. But these were the negative reasons. The much more powerful, positive, thing that drove me to join the Conservative Party was a desire for a deeper human connection to a country and its politics, mediated through an organisation whose values of hard work, education, enterprise, family and aspiration I shared.

This route to deepening a sense of belonging in an adoptive nation had been taken by some Ugandan Asians in Uganda before Amin's coup. Inspirational figures include Jayantbhai Madhvani (Manubhai's brother), who took a role in Milton Obote's government, and Mahendrabhai Mehta, who became a Ugandan MP and a special economic advisor to the government. However, for most Uganda Asians, political engagement was a complete unknown. We tended, wherever we settled in the world, to become entrenched in focusing solely on our communities and business activities. It would become my mission in life to help change that.

Through my grass-roots activity with the British Tories, I had met a lot of local Conservatives in Harrow and Barnet, together with significant figures in the wider party. Chief among these were Shantoo Ruparell in Harrow, whom I have mentioned, and Sir Jay Gohel, former chairman of the Anglo-Asian Conservative Party in Barnet. These two began the process of winning hundreds of thousands of Asian voters to the Tories, which has always been a major focus for me, too.

'We Asians are the original Conservatives because for thousands of years we have believed in free enterprise, freedom of the individual, private education and hard work; you have just stolen our philosophy,' Jay Gohel once joked to Margaret Thatcher, with whom he was good friends.

Although not primarily associated with British Indians in the public imagination, Mrs Thatcher had a great affection for us, I think. Finchley, her constituency in north London, was and remains home to a large number of British Indians.

It was in Finchley that I myself first met Mrs Thatcher, at a gathering of British Indians in a school hall in the summer of 1980. I had to work hard to get people to attend the event, even offering to pay for their bus fare, to ensure that we had a full hall – but we pulled it off. I look back now and cringe at the amateurism of it, but there we were, dozens of British Indians enthralled by our then Prime Minister. We felt important because this prominent politician wanted to meet us, and we'd never met any leaders in Uganda. In little over nine years we'd gone from Amin's terror to meeting the Prime Minister. Mrs Thatcher seemed nervous at first, but as she heard more and learned more, she seemed to realise that she had found herself among a group of shopkeepers to whom she could relate. She was marshalled around by Leslie Pym, the then leader of Barnet Council, and I remember just how statesmanlike she was.

Around the same time, British Indians also started to play a key role in holding on to councils in Brent and Harrow, which were majority Conservative until the early 1990s (Barnet remains Conservative).

I was one of a number of British Indians who was asked and encouraged to build an organisation that could create closer ties between the Conservative Party and our community. I took as my example the Prime Minister herself. I saw first-hand how Mrs Thatcher cared very deeply about her constituents in Finchley and was a great friend to us. She understood and admired the values of the first and second generation in the British Indian community, which are so often influenced by running family businesses – often small retail outlets that would have had a lot in common with the grocer's shop Mrs Thatcher's father ran in Grantham when she was a child.

You have to remember that Mrs Thatcher always saw herself as an outsider: she believed in the importance of individuals and families; she wanted to spread the benefits and advantages that had, for many years, been the privilege of the elite, and ensure as many people as possible received those benefits; and she had an outsider's desire to tackle institutions and elites that were withholding power from people. She was, in many ways, an anti-establishment Prime Minister.

Mrs Thatcher's political ethos appealed to many British Indians, as well as her commitment to family and wealth building. She made us realise that if you feel shut out, you yourself can act to change that. But many in the British Gujarati community at this time, if they were interested in politics at all, were seduced by the ideas of ethnic solidarity then promulgated by the Labour Party (which was also good at addressing individual communities and their issues). However, the Labour concept of subsuming every group into a single, homogenous social bloc was not the same as the active, patriotic individualism exemplified by Thatcher. Her attitude was better aligned with the spirit of enterprise that is at the heart not just of British Indian identity, but also of many immigrant identities, in my view.

Being a woman in politics was a big part of Thatcher's 'outsider-ness'. A female Prime Minister was a big change in many different ways and, I think, a challenge for many men. But her election was also a victory for meritocracy – for allowing the best person to get on with the job. I believe we all, especially in the British Indian community where the role of women has evolved so much in recent years, have a duty to encourage and to empower the new genera-tion of women, and that is especially true in politics. Our approach has been too old-fashioned. I am very pleased that slowly but surely the tide is turning, and there are now more and more role models for British Asian women who want to go into politics, including: Priti Patel, who was placed on the Conservative Party's 'A-List' of candidates and given a safe seat in the 2010 general election; Bar-oness Warsi; Baroness Verma; Baroness Vadera; and a new wave of women including Resham Kotecha, Councillor Meenal Sachdev, Councillor Mina Parmar and Councillor Reena Ranger.

David Cameron and I were always passionate about encouraging and empowering more women from ethnic minorities to get actively involved in politics and other areas of civic service. I still try to pro-mote this and, in March 2018, hosted the first International Women's Day debate in Parliament. It was the first time such a debate was hosted in the second chamber of the House of Lords for outside speakers. The event offered a tremendous platform for the empower-ment of all women, but British Indian women in particular.

Margaret Thatcher's premiership helped to reshape the UK's economy and give so many entrepreneurs a chance to grow their firms and thereby help the economy further. Mrs Thatcher's last-ing legacy for millions – including many British Indians across the country – was homeownership: the chance to become a property

ABOVE Dolar with Prime Minister John Major celebrating the tenth anniversary of the One Nation Forum in the Houses of Parliament.

LEFT Dolar with Manubhai Madhvani, his dear friend and mentor.

LEFT Morari Bapu with Dolar in London, a few days prior to Bapu's *Katha* (sacred Hindu texts) in Leicester.

Andrew Feldman, Sruti Dharma Das (the temple president) and Dolar at Bhaktivedanta Manor. The visit was part of Dolar's efforts to bring the Conservative Party closer to the British Indian community.

David Cameron lighting the candles at the first ever Conservative Party Diwali reception, organised by Dolar in 2009 – the largest Diwali function the party has ever hosted. Shailesh Vara (*far right*) looks on.

ABOVE Dolar's official introduction ceremony at the House of Lords with his family.
(*Left to right*: Rupeen, Sandhya, Dolar, his guru Morari Bapu, Shivaan and Paavan.)

LEFT A graphic illustration
of the Popat family coat
of arms. Its motto reads
'*Veritas Amor Compassio*', Latin
for 'Truth, love, compassion'.

Theresa May and the then president of the Hindu Forum of Britain, the late Arjan Vekaria, look on as Dolar speaks at a parliamentary Diwali reception, 2009.

LEFT Dolar with Paavan and Rupeen at Morari Bapu's *Katha* on Mount Kailash, one of the holiest sites in Hinduism.

Dolar and Sandhya with David and Samantha Cameron at a reception at Woburn Abbey in 2011.

Prominent Indian Cabinet minister Smriti Irani presenting David Cameron with a Ganesh *murti* (idol) at Dolar's launch of the Conservative Friends of India in April 2012. Sandhya's uncle, Ramesh Sachdev, is on the left.

Dolar accompanying Prime Minister David Cameron to the Neasden Temple – one of the largest Hindu temples in the UK – for Diwali celebrations in 2013 as part of his engagement with the British Indian community.

David Cameron's trade delegation touches down in India. (*Back row*: David Willetts and Dolar. *Middle row*: Asha Khemka and Priti Patel.)

ABOVE The House of Lords Conservative
whips during the coalition government.

LEFT Her Majesty's official guests:
Dolar and Sandhya with Sheila
and Kamlesh Madhvani in the
Royal Enclosure at Royal Ascot, 2013.

LEFT Dolar speaking at the St Luke's Hospice
reception at No. 10, as Samantha Cameron
looks on. They had worked together to
organise the event.

LEFT Dolar representing the British government on royal duties with the Countess of Wessex, at the funeral of President Sata of Zambia in 2014.

BELOW The Queen's royal car picking up Dolar outside The Knoll, on his way to receive the President of Tanzania, Jakaya Kikwete.

Dolar meeting Indian Prime Minister Narendra Modi in 2014 ahead of the Indian election.

PHOTO COURTESY OF SMRITI IRANI.

owner and invest in your family's future, which appealed to our community's traditional values of family and aspiration. We owe our first female Prime Minister so much for helping to build a country that gave people opportunities and challenged the decline that Britain faced in the late 1970s. People forget this now, especially the young, who have no idea of how tough things were then, with very few jobs, high prices and interest rates, and what felt like strikes happening every five minutes.

By tackling the excessive powers of trade unions – which had caused so much damage to previous governments – Mrs Thatcher helped to create an environment in which businesses could flourish. I would never argue that defeating the unions was without significant negative impact on many people, but it did help to restore order and democratic accountability to this great country.

It would, in time, be a slightly surreal experience for me to meet Baroness Thatcher in the House of Lords: the Iron Lady, no longer so sure on her feet, but with the same fighting spirit.

The efforts of Jay Gohel and Shantoo Ruparell, along with my own work, had a deep impact on the Conservative Party, and contributed to its electoral victories in 1983, 1987 and 1992. But there was still an awful lot of work to do in getting out the British Indian vote. I committed myself to electioneering on behalf of local candidates in Harrow and also became active in the Anglo-Asian Conservative Association, which Gohel founded and of which I later became secretary for four years.

It was in these experiences that my political identity and social conscience were forged – here and at home with Sandhya and the children, and in my many years of contact with my guru, Morari Bapu.

We had made so many mistakes in Uganda. In smaller rural areas the Ugandan Asians were part of the community's fabric, but in larger towns we were outsiders. People perceived us as rich, even though it was often untrue. I think we *were* often racist to the black Africans around us, treating them badly and stirring resentment, but perhaps our greatest mistake was ignoring the political process. We chose to get on with our businesses and day-to-day lives, and neglected the national conversation. This created an inbuilt hatred for us in the African community. In Britain we had to avoid making the same mistakes we'd made in east Africa, by embracing the country that we now called home, turning up the volume on our Britishness and trying and educate others about who we were and where we'd come from.

For myself, I have never seen a contradiction between being British, Hindu, Gujarati and east African, all at the same time. But if one has accepted the benefits and rights of being a British citizen, and a subject of the sovereign, along with all that is entailed by being represented in the British Parliament and protected by the British state, one's British identity must be the primary one, politically speaking. In my mind, there is no question that my nationality comes before my faith or country of origin; it was why I was so keen later on to get the British Hindu Forum to adopt the slogan: 'Proud to be British, Proud to be Hindu.'

I accepted the importance of asserting a genuine loyalty to Britain almost the first day I arrived here, and that recognition lies at the heart of any advice I would presume to pass on to future immigrants to Britain and to those struggling to reconcile being British with their ethnicity, or any other aspect of their identity. I think of it in relation to grammar: you have to learn to embrace the hyphen – or hyphens – of your multifaceted ethnic status, but make sure that the main verb of your identity is being British. So you might be a British-Indian person or a British-Indian-Ugandan person, but you must still say definitively, 'I am British.' It's a matter of actualising identity in the widest sense, of being true to yourself, with all your mixed-up DNA and experience, but also being loyal to the context in which you find yourself. I truly believe that some of this actualisation of identity should involve political action, whether you are on the left, the right or, like so many British people, some-where in between.

In the Anglo-Asian Conservative Association, it was my job to organise functions with MPs, Cabinet ministers and members of the Asian community, to enable the latter group to participate in political processes from which they were often excluded, or had excluded themselves.

I met my first Member of Parliament in 1980: Rhodes Boyson, MP for Brent North. Then a Conservative stronghold, this seat was lost in the Labour landslide in 1997 and has never been recovered since (my parliamentary assistant, Ameet Jogia, would go on to stand in the seat for the Conservatives in the 2017 general election, representing a new generation of British-born Indian politicians).

There has always been a common misconception that the Con-servative Party is a racist party. However, we east African Indians – many of whom are Conservative voters – would never tolerate any form of organisational racism given the circumstances in which we came to this country. But, this misunderstanding about 'racist Conservatives' created a mistrust that prevented many Indians from joining the party and indeed often drove them into the arms of Labour.

This mistrust was partly to do with the wider social picture. Racism was rife in the 1970s; I experienced it many times myself. When I was younger, my brother and I were refused entry to play snooker in a pub, despite having paid up front. Regrettably, racism will almost certainly *always* be around, but we can't brand the Conservative Party as racist. Being sensible on immigration isn't racist; it's a view held by many – if not most – British Indians. But in the 1970s, when we'd only recently moved here and still felt vulnerable, hearing politicians talk about 'controlling immigration' came across as, 'We don't like you or want you here.' It wasn't until we entered the new millennium that this feeling really started to dissipate.

I joined the Conservative Party despite this public misconception. I was one of the first British Indians to do so. Only by being at the heart of the issue can you influence change – that was my belief. I wanted to try and change minds, to educate those within the party: 'These are our values; they're the same as yours.' It was often slow going. At countless events, I'd go along and find myself on the table furthest away from the centre of the room (this only really changed during David Cameron's leadership). But I never gave up. Now the overwhelming majority of British Indians would recognise these same trends that align us to the Conservative Party. It is our natural home.

During the 1980s and 1990s I successfully organised receptions with Virginia Bottomley (as Health Secretary), Cecil Parkinson (as party chairman) and Michael Portillo (as Employment Secretary) – and not forgetting, of course, Margaret Thatcher and John Major as successive Prime Ministers. I briefly met Mr Major at a party conference in the late 1980s, and in 1989 he attended a reception that Sandhya and I held at our home. Two weeks later, Major was made Foreign Secretary and, in 1991, the working-class boy from Brixton went on to become Prime Minister.

Major was the first to recognise that the Conservatives didn't just need to engage British Indians, but needed to make sure that they were not discriminated against within the party. 'I have never been a victim of racial discrimination, but any decent person would agree that those kinds of acts are utterly repugnant in a civilised nation like Britain. They have no place in our country and never in our party,' he said during a speech welcoming the contributions of British Asians at a rally at the Commonwealth Institute in January 1997. This event marked the fiftieth anniversary of the independence of India and Pakistan and both Hindus and Muslims were amply represented.

Afterwards, Kalpesh Solanki and I presented Major with a wreath and a copy of *Garavi Gujarat*, one of the main magazines for the Gujarati community in Britain, of which Kalpesh was managing editor and to which I remain a frequent contributor (I also used to write a regular column for the newspaper *Asian Voice*, which was owned by my good friend C. B. Patel).

By the late 1990s, my grass-roots work was taking up more and more time. I was chairman of the Stanmore Park Ward of the Conservative Party, a post I held for four years, and president of Harrow East Conservative Association. I have also been a member of both the British Asian Conservative Link and the Conservative Ethnic Diversity Council. What began with Mrs Thatcher's understated empathy with the community became, under John Major, a commitment to substantive action, as the Conservative Party developed an appetite for engaging with the British Indian community.

Part of this shift was the result of a body developed under Major that went beyond bringing British Indians into the Tory fold. The One Nation Forum gathers together Conservative representatives from all minority groups to ensure that the party is aware of their interests, and also encourages the growth of BME membership in constituency associations. A direct result of this work must be the fact that a number of Conservative MPs in densely populated ethnic minority constituencies have increased their share of the vote in the past three elections.

The One Nation Forum was committed to equality of opportunity in politics, believing ethnic minority candidates should be selected for seats based on their ability, competence and merit, as well as a long and proven long history of work, particularly at grassroots level. I served as chair of the One Nation Forum's Barnet and Harrow branch, of which John Major was a big supporter; he hosted the organisation's tenth anniversary at the House of Commons in February 1997. Again, his speech at that event was addressed as much to the party as to the country. He said, 'No one is disbarred from playing a full part in the Conservative Party; if you have the ability and the conviction, that is all we ask.' The reason this is important is that there was still some residual racism among individual Tories that wouldn't really be flushed out until David Cameron became leader. His success in doing so would be a contributing factor in the emergence of UKIP (as was the failure of Labour to adequately engage working-class communities).

Also in this period, I was first vice chair and then chairman of the Strangers' Gallery, a private parliamentary club for the business community of Harrow. It was always one of my favourite gatherings. In the early 1990s, the Strangers' Gallery provided a forum for local businesspeople to meet and not only enjoy some convivial company, but also to discuss matters of political significance. The crossover between politics and business has a murky reputation, but the impact government policy has on businesses is so profound that I've always felt it is essential that these sort of groups exist, to allow politicians and business leaders the opportunity to develop an understanding. Even now I spend a lot of time encouraging MPs to establish business clubs, because otherwise politicians can be too hasty in assuming they know the consequences of their actions.

The late Baroness Miller was our Speaker in January 1997, filling us with enthusiasm for the general election battle that was fast approaching. Then the Rt Hon. Francis Maude hosted an excellent evening at the Cavendish Pavilion in the summer of 1997.

We were all naturally disappointed that our efforts were thrown into confusion by Tony Blair's victory in May that year. Blair was very much modelled on American politicians. He was a good mouthpiece, and a brilliant actor and orator. He could show his emotions easily and even his body language convinced people how genuine he was. He won three elections on this basis. Any politician could learn something from him.

Engaging with people is very important in politics these days. My memory of Edward Heath, Harold Wilson, James Callaghan, Margaret Thatcher and John Major was that they were all rather cautious, formal people. They kept their distance with the public and did not engage with people as much as Blair did, or Cameron later on. Some of the problems that Theresa May faced in the 2017 election are associated with this issue. She clearly realised this and made attempts to address the problem.

Two decades earlier, business clubs such as the Strangers' Club were beginning to allow many British Indians to find a foothold in the Conservative Party. What was driving these clubs' activities (and mine) was a belief that the Tory Party, rather than Labour, is the right place for all those people of immigrant descent who believe in the same things that the Conservative Party believes in: family, community, hard work, education, freedom, enterprise, self-reliance and social responsibility. For as many years as I can remember, I have worked to achieve a deeper and more sustained engagement between the Conservative Party and Asian communities as well as other minority groups, especially in marginal seats.

In the late 1990s, there wasn't just a need to educate Britain's immigrant populations about the opportunities open to them as members of the Conservative Party; there was also a need to educate the party itself. We needed to persuade some of our members that minority communities and groups are part of the lifeblood of Conservatism, rather than a bloc against which Conservatism defines itself (a negative characterisation we have recently seen in the unpleasant rhetoric of UKIP). I was lucky to find allies not just in ethnic leadership, such as Jay Gohel, but also in the higher echelons of the Tory Party. One of my happiest memories was receiving John Major along with Gohel at my house at Stanmore during the '90s and presenting him with a traditional Hindu wreath. Major was accompanied that day by Hugh, now Lord, Dykes, who was formerly an MP for Harrow East (1970–97).

Slowly, during the Blair years, attitudes to immigrant communities began to change among the Tories, but it was an uphill battle to get people to commit to brokering formal relationships. For a long time our party was its own worst enemy when dealing with the Hindu community.

Blair made the running on the inclusion of members of Britain's ethnic minority communities in Cabinet, appointing such figures as Paul Boating, Baroness Amos and Baroness Scotland. I think David Cameron learned a valuable lesson from him in this, as in other respects.

By the time Gordon Brown became Prime Minister in 2007, the Labour Party had a dedicated taskforce that had been set up to keep in touch with prominent Hindu community members. Brown even sent people Diwali greetings and Christmas cards. Protesting that these voters were natural Tories, I began suggesting to fellow Conservatives that we must formulate a better strategy on how the party was to galvanise Hindu voters.

'British Indian votes are soft votes, votes for grabs!' I used to say to party activists and MPs. What I meant was that British Indians are rational and flexible; we respond to attention and to reasoned argument as much as to what is in our own interest.

My nascent plans included getting leading Tories attending three or four annual Hindu functions. My home turf would play a big role in this. The London Borough of Harrow has a 29 per cent Hindu population, the largest in the UK. But Indians live in marginal constituencies all over Britain.

Between 1997 and 2005, I devoted vast amounts of time to getting out the British Indian vote. I spent a lot of time mentoring prospective candidates in constituencies with large Indian minorities, as well as getting involved in a range of initiatives that supported diversity in the Conservative Party in other ways.

People interpret the word 'diversity' in different ways. To me, diversity means people from all communities should feel a sense of pride in being British without feeling they have to leave their traditions behind.

I adore the diversity found in Britain, from the different street cuisines to the festivals that light up our high streets. Yet I have always thought that, in return for this variety, we must respect and adopt the British values, traditions and culture around us. This is the sort of tolerant and inclusive Britain we want, not communities living separate lives, isolating themselves and their children. When all communities come together, barriers come down and diversity can be truly celebrated.

8

THE CAMERON ERA BEGINS

W hen David Cameron became leader of the Conservatives in 2005, I wrote to him at once to say that I felt winning the British Indian vote was a priority, and to offer my services. We met and got on extremely well, and he was soon doing things such as mentioning Diwali in Parliament and visiting the Hare Krishna Temple in Hertsmere (his first official event involving the Hindu community).

The same year, Shailesh Vara, the newly elected Member of Parliament for North West Cambridgeshire, organised for Cameron to attend a function at the Soar Valley Community College in Leicester. Another Ugandan Asian immigrant and a long-term friend, Shailesh had already served as vice chairman of the Conservative Party and would later become Parliamentary Under-Secretary of State at the Ministry of Justice and Minister of State for Northern Ireland. At this gathering in Leicester, my guru, Morari Bapu, was reciting 'Ramkatha' (excerpts from the Hindu epic *Ramayana*). This event attracted a large number of Bapu's followers from around the country, with around 5,000 in the live audience. It offered a major platform for Cameron to appeal for support from Britain's Hindu community.

Why did David Cameron's speech hit home that day? I think because it tapped into the belief of many Hindus that the Hindu community had, unlike other faith groups, been taken for granted by the three main parties. He strove hard to convey the message that he was aware of the problems faced by the community and that he would be the right person to deal with them.

Cameron also personally met many Hindus that day. Before his speech, in a one-to-one chat, I had given him the advice that all he needed to do was 'give us Hindus a smile', and he obliged. He really liked to chat, in fact, and engage with people on a personal level, which is an important quality in a politician. In that way Cameron is, as many have remarked, more like Blair than some of his Conservative predecessors as Prime Minister.

In 2007, David Cameron and I met up 'outside school' at a dinner party at the splendid house of the businessman and philanthropist Paul (now Sir Paul) Ruddock, where we had a very informative discussion on various party policies.

During our talk, I suggested that party policy include a mortgage guarantee scheme for either first-time buyers who are engaged or young married couples, but most of our exchange was about how to make further inroads into the Hindu community. As a follow-up I sent Cameron a list of things we needed to do to win the British Indian vote. I don't think either of us would realise how far that process would extend beyond the forthcoming election, or how close we would become personally while we worked on it.

Many people during this period said to me, 'Dolar, you do so much for the party, why don't you stand as an MP yourself?' They would cite the example of Shailesh Vara. Like me, Shailesh had been involved with the Conservative Party since the 1983 election and held various posts at local, regional and national level before entering Parliament, including being a member of the Anglo-Asian Conservatives when I was the group's leader.

Yes, I thought about standing as a candidate, even getting the requisite papers together – but something held me back. Despite my success in business, and in engaging ethnic minorities with Conservatism, I still somehow lacked confidence.

Some of this was to do with language – not just my ability to promote my own qualities but also being sure of myself grammatically. Although friends will joke that I can talk them under the table, I feel I'm not great with words; I suffer from dyslexia, and have done so since I was a child. I could not read until I was ten and developed terrible handwriting (it's still pretty bad), partly as a consequence of being forced to write with my right hand when I wanted to write with my left. Being tortured so much by Grewal at school hadn't helped, obviously. For some reason, even though I was now a successful businessman with a happy family, I still felt as if I was in disgrace. It was almost as if I felt I didn't deserve to be an MP.

Foolish thinking, of course, but my brothers and sisters know what I am talking about. When I look back through photographs, there is one of me sitting on a climbing frame aged fourteen, in the grounds of Rock View School, with Tororo Rock in the background. I am alone and staring into the sky. I look anxious, as if I am waiting for news of another failed test to be delivered to my parents or waiting to face another thrashing from Grewal. Or perhaps I am thinking of the future and that whatever happens in it, however I try to make the best of it as it unfolds, Dolar the failure, Dolar the chancer, Dolar the quick-buck guy, is going to make a mess of it.

Something of this, some idea that I would colossally fail, held me back from standing as an MP. However, the reasons were not only negative. I also had other political priorities, chief among them a commitment to promoting community cohesion. The fact is, I enjoyed being an activist. It may be only the first step on the political ladder, but it's where I was happy to be; I enjoyed the work and being part of the team. It's very important to me, this idea that political activism gets you closer to the decision-making process, so you can influence it. Another reason not to stand was that I don't believe you can fully separate business and politics.

Although I am not a believer in caste (except in its positive, identity-enhancing aspects), I must say that this notion of community activism is one very much associated with the *Lohana*, of which I am a part. Many *Lohanas* feel, like me, that they cannot separate business and politics, but often commit to doing a form of work that benefits the community.

For me, it has all been about extending that *Lohana* belief in service into a wider conception of community cohesion and action, focusing on the idea that different cultures can be reconciled and united inside the framework of Britain's democratic process. This is a different concept to multiculturalism, as I shall try to explain.

So my political activity was to take a form other than being an MP and much of the reason was to do with my relationship with David Cameron; meeting each other on a monthly basis, we went on to form a strong bond.

Like me (but unlike some Tories), Cameron was and is a One Nation Conservative. When he was Prime Minister, he understood instinctively that minority communities were key to the new type of Conservatism that he wanted to foster, and I fell into place as someone who could help him make that happen. (In general, British ethnic minorities are playing an increasingly significant role in the development of One Nation Conservatism, which historically was involved in linking rich and poor and north and south, as an alternative to socialism.)

During 2007, Andrew Feldman – the Conservative Party's chief executive (and later its chairman) – David Cameron and I developed a plan to persuade more British Indians (who, as I have described, were often reluctant to support the party in the past) that the values they hold most dear strongly overlap with those expressed by modern Conservatism. At our first meeting, I stressed the same advice I had given Cameron during our one-to-one before Bapu's recital in Leicester, telling Andrew that the Conservatives have the right policies but the wrong approach to our community. The success of the Labour Party involved their engagement with the British Indian community – they would always address our gatherings and interact so well and they understood the issues our community were facing. The Conservatives were completely out of touch on this, I told him.

Other ventures I suggested to help guarantee a Tory victory in the next general election included: engaging with the Asian media, the *Asian Voice* and the *Eastern Eye*; a dinner hosted by David Cameron with prominent Asian business people; a breakfast and seminar in a London hotel for prospective Conservative parliamentary candidates in ethnically-rich marginal seats, so I and others could explain to them what they needed to do to win; a visit by David Cameron to address the audience at the enormous Swaminarayan Hindu Temple in Neasden; a reception with the then shadow Health Secretary, Andrew Lansley, for Asian doctors and dentists; and a forum on immigration that invited lawyers and academics from the Asian community to discuss ideas with the shadow Attorney General (this event took place because most Asians who have lived in Britain for many years don't like to see large numbers of immigrants).

Some of my plans were put into action, some weren't (or were implemented only after the election in 2010 had been won). That is the nature of a political campaign, which is always hovering between hope and achievability, with the clock always loudly ticking down to the day when the polling stations open.

In the autumn of 2007, we didn't actually know for certain when the next battle to win votes would officially start. The day could have come sooner, had Gordon Brown called a snap general election, which of course he should have done. He probably would have won.

In the period from 2007 to 2008, the worst economic crisis of modern times also coincided with a banking crisis. My TLC Group was largely unaffected by this because of my liquidity rule, but I was very worried that the Bank of Scotland would recall their loan for the Holiday Inn we were planning to build on the site we owned in Luton, which would have made things very difficult. With respect to the fortunes of the wider British Indian community in this economic climate, I felt that because we always all helped each other, we would be able to trade our way out of it. I told both David Cameron and Andrew Feldman this and they were happy to hear it.

The financial crisis was bad for the Tory image, however. At this time there was perhaps still an impression in Britain that the Conservative Party was closely associated with the City of London and was therefore responsible for what was going wrong in the economy. Going into 2009, the party's problems segued into unrelated territory – namely the Eton/Oxford image problem of Johnson, Osborne and Cameron, and the parliamentary expenses scandal – but all these things risked coming together in a chain in the public mind.

The expenses scandal was a big deal, but it got overblown. In my own view, only four or five of those charged were truly corrupt. Many of the others had made petty mistakes. Although it is crucial to have clear ethical and financial standards in civic life and be transparent about these, there is a danger of us losing perspective. I think that compared to those in the rest of the world, Britain's democracy is very clean.

During 2009, my discussions with Cameron and Feldman led to one of the events I've most enjoyed being involved in over the past thirty-six years. I don't care if it sounds like boasting: it was a definitive triumph, changing the nature of relations between Tories and British Indians for good.

This event was the first ever Diwali celebration to be held at Conservative Party headquarters, then at 30 Millbank. It took place on Friday 16 October: the eve of Diwali. One of the most popular festivals of the Hindu faith, Diwali spiritually signifies the victory of light over darkness, good over evil, knowledge over ignorance and hope over despair.

I did most of the organising for the event, working in conjunction with Andrew Feldman. I hired Altitude, the event space at the top of Millbank Tower, and set about inviting 900 members of the Hindu community from across the country.

The usually modern-looking Altitude space was transformed into what one guest dubbed 'a Palace in Rajasthan', with food and décor to match. My sons Rupeen and Paavan and my wife Sandhya did an amazing job in helping bringing it together. Cameron, then still Leader of the Opposition, made a brilliant address to the room, which was filled with Asian faces from banking, the law, the media and industry.

The evening at Millbank was a major event for the community. The British Indian media was shocked that I had organised an event of this nature; there had never been one that big, nor had there been one organised by the Conservative Party for its British Indian members. It was also a big moment for David Cameron. On the night, he was his usual well-turned-out self: tall, slim and wearing a smart suit with a blue tie. I sensed there was a slight nervousness underneath the surface, as if he was unsure of what to make of the overwhelming Indian ambience, with all its bright colours and sensory power, but he grew in confidence as the night went on, perhaps recognising, even as it was happening, that the event represented a real breakthrough.

Cameron began his speech that night with the words, 'Diwali is for all of you,' meaning the Hindus present. He then continued:

But the themes of the festival are relevant to everyone: truth, hope, friendship, optimism, a fresh start and thorough spring clean. We could do with a bit of that in Britain – and we need to start just down the road in Parliament. But this is a good time for thinking about the change we need in this country.

He went on to speak of commonalities between British and Hindu values, touching on the many topics he and I had discussed with Andrew Feldman in the preceding years. By the end of this speech, Cameron was being acclaimed by enthusiastic members of the audience.

Afterwards I received hundreds of emails saying what a good time had been had, including this instructive missive: 'DC was like a film star – I could not believe the scrum that surrounded him. I once attended a Conservative Asian link event with Iain Duncan Smith in north London. Gosh how the mood has changed since those difficult days!'

Cameron also attended another recital by Bapu in 2009, this time at Wembley Arena. His office had initially declined the invitation as it was close to the Norwich North by-election, but I mentioned it to him over a lunch and he immediately accepted. His speech at Wembley was a big success for him and I believe his biggest breakthrough with the British Indian community. The event was televised live worldwide, reaching even vaster audiences of around four million. Cameron was now becoming a bit like a rock star among the British Indian community, and his status in India also grew (which helped when he visited there on matters of state after becoming Prime Minister).

It is pretty remarkable that all this was happening as David was caring for his young, disabled son, Ivan. We all knew it was only a matter of time before Ivan's dreadful illness took him away from David and Samantha, and this sadly happened, very suddenly, in February 2009. I remembered seeing Ivan at their house when Sandhya and I attended a dinner reception there, and also met him on another occasion. It was obvious that he was a happy child surrounded by love and cherished by his parents.

That same year, as the Camerons balanced public triumphs and personal tragedy, I was lucky enough to be honoured at the Asian Political and Public Life Awards by the Conservative Party's then chairman, Eric Pickles, for my work promoting the party in the British Indian community. I was pleased about this and genuinely happy that the Conservative Party was becoming more diverse and representative of the country at large. But the journey was by no means over.

The election was coming up in May 2010. There was lots of work to do. It seems bizarre to think of it now, but at the time the Conservatives had not won an election since 1992. I knocked on lots of doors and wrote a lot of newspaper articles for the British Indian press, trying to mobilise support in every way I could think of. While Cameron had taken John Major's efforts at understanding our community and super-sized them, developing a real relationship between the Conservative Party and the British Indians, it still needed to filter down to those on the ground. I spent a considerable time coaching candidates for both Parliament and council elections on how to engage with ethnic minorities.

I spent the election campaign itself largely in Harrow East (a Labour seat since 1997), holding events and making calls to support the Conservative candidate, Bob Blackman.

It was during this time, on 19 November 2009, that David Cameron nominated me for a life peerage. On the day the call came, I was attending a friend's daughter's wedding at the Grove Hotel in Watford. We had stayed overnight at the hotel. I remember the day being a little windy. I received a call at 10.50 a.m., ten minutes before the wedding was going to start, on the hotel's lawn. I rushed to get the phone, conscious I didn't have much time.

A voice said on the phone, 'Dolar, it's David here.'

I said, 'David who?'

'David Cameron,' he chuckled.

As usual, my confidence escaped me. He'd never phoned me in person before. I started feeling nervous, sure that something had gone wrong.

'Dolar,' he said, 'we have been so happy with all the work you have done, we would like to make you a peer.'

Frankly speaking, I had no idea what he meant. Unsure what to say, I responded with, 'Well, we've got a lot of work to do if we want to win the election.'

As usual, David was unflustered. 'Dolar, when we win the election, I would like you to be a part of our team in Westminster, supporting the government.'

The penny dropped. I was stunned. It was a surreal moment and all I remember is saying something again about the potential of the Conservative Party to engage with the British Indian community.

That same night, Sandhya and I were attending a dinner at a stately home. Cameron was present, as was John Major. Lord Strathclyde, leader of the Conservatives in the Lords, was seated next to Sandhya for what felt like an informal interview. I remember that night very clearly. There was a moment of recognition, or self-realisation, which went off like a flash bulb in my consciousness: I'd not only been accepted, I'd become part of the core team at the heart of the Conservative Party. I'd worked for thirty years to try to make it possible for others to take this path – but suddenly I realised I had walked up it myself.

Later, in the formal letter of notification, Cameron wrote to me explaining that we shared a determination to find new ways of doing things, giving people real responsibility and power, adding that he was impressed with the work I had done so far.

That letter was followed by one from Lord Strathclyde, inviting me to attend a preparatory meeting. Although I had received the notification letter before it, I was completely shocked to receive this invitation; the whole thing still didn't feel real. I was also shocked to hear that following the nomination I would be subject to a vetting process by the House of Lords Appointments Commission, and even more so to hear that the nomination would then need to be accepted by Her Majesty the Queen. It would take me three months to accept. I wasn't sure I was worthy of the role, and Sandhya wasn't sure either. She had never wanted me to be a politician or to ever stand for Parliament, and didn't relish the idea of her husband being a Lord. In the end, she very reluctantly had to step into public life, but after I had accepted the invitation she was fully supportive.

It was only after I got the blessing of my guru, Morari Bapu, that I felt able to accept; he characterised the peerage as a form of communal, even religious, service. He also said that I should see the House of Lords as a kind of temple, and I really liked that idea.

The House of Lords is, in fact, the best kind of temple: one that takes account of both knowledge and the experience of older people, and by and large it really does ameliorate the work of Parliament. In a way it is all the more remarkable that I characterise the Lords in this way because in the main I am against building temples, with regards to the habit that Hindus and other religious followers have of pledging private wealth to fund new places of worship. My feeling is that we must change our giving habits, moving from donations to help build temples to using newly acquired wealth to shape society. I'll write more about philanthropy elsewhere, but I tarry here only to say that I feel that the Lords, for all its faults, really does help British society.

As part of the vetting process for the role, I had to declare whether I had made donations to any political party – of course I had, consistently giving some of my income to the Conservative Party over the previous thirty years. It was not a sudden thing, this financial support for the Tories, though I would have a hard time persuading a reporter that this was the case.

It must have been the day before the peerage was to be announced in June 2010. I was in the kitchen. We were about to sit down – the family and Sandhya's aunt, Pravina, who was visiting from Toronto – to a traditional Gujarati dish, such as a *rotlo* or *khichdi*, when the phone rang. I went to answer it.

A voice said, 'Is that Dolar Popat?'

I said, 'Yes, who's there?'

It was a journalist from a major British newspaper.

'We believe you've given £200,000 to the Conservative Party, hence you've got a peerage,' said the voice on the other end of the phone.

A little stunned by this full-frontal approach, I replied, 'You're half right, half wrong.'

'What do you mean?'

I told him, 'I've got the peerage, yes. But the amount of money you are quoting is not correct.'

He said, 'Well, surely you gave money.'

'Yes,' I replied, 'but you've got your figures wrong. Where did you get them?'

'Public sources.'

'I see. Well, they are wrong for all that.'

'Can you tell me the right ones?'

'That's not my job. That's your job to find out.'

He tried a few numbers, as if he were a bingo caller, getting crosser and crosser as I rejected each one.

And in the end, I said, 'You're not right, I'm afraid. So I can't talk much with you.'

Then he asks me another question, getting quite angry as he demanded, 'Are you saying that you haven't given any money to the Conservative Party?'

I replied, 'Of course I've given money! In fact, I've given substantially more than you're quoting! And am very proud to have done so. If you do your research and get your facts right and give me the correct figures, I'll be very happy to speak to you.'

He never called back.

When my peerage was announced in June, the paper led with the headline: 'Tycoon who gave Tories £200k nominated for a peerage by David Cameron'. Within the first three paragraphs, the article used the dreaded phrase 'cash for peerages'. I'd never really dealt with the press before, so this was a baptism by fire.

I toughened up a bit later in dealing with the media, but at the time I felt a bit stung by this. As I explained, I have been a financial contributor to the Conservative Party since 1980: paying for events; sponsoring functions at party conferences; holding events at my own house for MPs to meet members of the British Indian community; and yes, giving financial donations. I've never made a secret of that, but people assume it to be a cause of shame. Far from it: I'm very proud to be able to financially support the political party I believe in. I never expected or asked for anything in return.

My origins are relevant here, as I am hardly an example of the traditional parodic image of a Tory: the gammon-faced English businessman who has had everything on a plate since he was a public schoolboy and now fancies a lordship. By contrast, when I came to this country, I had nothing. It was the most Christian of acts to welcome me here and allow me to make a living, and that same version of 'helping thy neighbour' was extended to thousands of my fellow Ugandan Asians. The government responsible for this generous act was a Conservative one, under Ted Heath. It was a move that was strongly opposed by other political forces at the time.

Is it any surprise that I want to repay an organisation that gave me the greatest gift I have received in my life? I feel I have a duty to give back to my country, and that the best way of doing so is through supporting – with time, effort and money – that same political party.

However, I am aware there are big questions about political party funding that need to be addressed. I am aware that financial support of this kind often inspires suspicion and can erode trust in the democratic process. I have an open mind about whether some degree of public funding for political parties would help, but we certainly need to find ways to restore faith in the system.

What I would say is that democratic political action at party level does not come cheap. In an ideal world, the membership of each party would be so numerous that their flat-rate annual subscription of £25 would finance all the usual activities, including election campaigns and the salaries of the permanent staff in the respective party headquarters. Alas, we do not live in that ideal world (or even in a nearby galaxy).

In countries such as the UK, which have traditionally eschewed payments to political parties from the public purse, those parties have been obliged to seek donations from other sources above and beyond member subscriptions. The cost of running a major political party is significant – in the case of the Conservative Party, it is currently at least £15 million a year. Membership subscriptions probably bring in around £1 million, so the considerable shortfall comes from donations from people like myself, money raised at the party conference or at major social events like the Black and White Ball, and smaller fundraising drives.

Donations made by rich – and often powerful – people have led to a number of controversies and uncertainty about the levels of influence secured by the donors. In my own case, I know it's not just journalists who have criticised me – members of the British Indian community have done so too. But in the context of my other charitable donations, the amount I have given the Conservative Party is negligible.

I do believe that freedom, the rule of law and upholding democracy don't come cheap. You only have to look at how much is spent on a presidential election in the USA, or see the violence that is associated with so many elections in the developing world, to realise how our situation is so much better than others.

9

IN AT THE DEEP END

The 2010 British general election was held on Thursday 6 May. None of the parties achieved the 326 seats needed for an overall majority. Led by David Cameron, the Conservative Party won the largest number of votes and seats, but was still twenty seats short of being able to form a government. This hung Parliament resulted in the Conservatives having to form a coalition with the Liberal Democrats, led by Nick Clegg. As Cameron took office as Prime Minister, I reflected on what it meant for British Indians – and for me, given that in July I would be taking my seat in the House of Lords.

Meanwhile, analysis of how the result came about started in earnest across the media. Some of the contributory factors were easy to identify, such as the frailty of the economy and strength of David Cameron's leadership qualities. But one shift in electoral behaviour slipped through the pundits' net: the fact that the British Indian community had come out in force to support the Conservative Party. Marginal constituencies in London – such as Harrow East (where Bob Blackman won), Hendon, Finchley and Golders Green, Ealing Central and Acton, and Brentford and Isleworth – all saw huge increases in the proportion of British Indians who had put a cross in the box for the Tories.

The Conservative Party has always felt like home to me. As a community, we British Indians are natural Conservatives. While the 2010 election result was a tremendous achievement in terms of the largest number of British Indians ever voting for the Tories, it seemed strange that it had taken so long.

Cameron was the first Conservative leader to fully commit to engaging with the British Indian community and to take us seriously. He recognised the rewards that this engagement would bring – not just electorally, but also for the country. The result of the 2010 general election was therefore a pivotal moment for the community, but deep down I knew that we could do more, and that we still had a long way to go.

The 2010 campaign was the eighth election campaign I'd contributed to as an activist, and I'd worked for over thirty years to try to bridge the gap between my political party and my community. It seemed that this time, finally, something had shifted.

After Gordon Brown resigned following the election, it was striking that so many of the potential leaders of the Labour Party came out and identified that it was not the party of aspiration, which is one of the values that British Indians value so highly. It seemed, on the basis of this, and a focus on other common values such as entrepreneurship and community, that the relationship between British Indians and the Conservatives would only strengthen.

That said, I had become convinced in the run-up to the 2010 election that parties should stop issuing community-specific manifestos (separate versions of the Conservative Party's document had been written for the Sikh, Jewish and Muslim communities).

I found this troubling; I see the Conservatives as a family made up of different ethnicities, and I think we should present ourselves in a unified manner. Publishing separate manifestos divided us. We should be basing our strategy on what is best for the country, not on what promises we can extract from politicians on the basis of skin colour or creed.

People seem, at times of political stress, to forget that they can have many identities. Politically it is almost always best to focus on territory where as many points intersect as possible – for most of us, this is British citizenship, with all the rights, privileges and opportunities that it entails.

The tension between regional, ethnic and religious identities, as well as a pluralist concept of national unity would be major themes in my maiden speech in the Lords. But before making it, I had to go through an induction process, part of which involved selecting a coat of arms for myself. At first, this antiquated procedure seemed a long way from modern Britain and my own concerns. Coats of arms were traditionally used in battle to enable soldiers to see where their leaders were, so, bold and full of colour, they were designed to be eye-catching and impressive.

My coat of arms was designed in consultation with my guru, Morari Bapu, the College of Arms (Britain's official heraldic authority) and my family. Its motto reads '*Veritas Amor Compassio*': Latin for 'truth, love and compassion' (as mentioned, the phrase that inspired the name of my business, which came from the teachings of Bapu).

The focal point of the design of my coat of arms is Hanuman, the Hindu deity central to the *Ramayana*, the text that inspires so many of Bapu's teachings. The depiction exactly replicates the statue of Hanuman crafted for Bapu in his home town of Mahuva, Gujarat (where he celebrates Hanuman's birthday every year). As with the original statue, Hanuman is shown with a *Shivling* behind him (a holy symbol depicting Lord Shiva).

The left support is a female *Gir* cow, symbolising my ancestral home in Gujarat, where *Gir* cows are found. The right support is an African lion symbolising my birth in Africa. Both animals are shown in their natural colours (which is unusual for heraldry), to reflect the importance of nature to me, and the animals are shown to be at peace with one another, to underline the pacifist nature of Hinduism. The crest (the element on top of the helmet) is a depiction of Mount Kailash in Tibet. Kailash was chosen because of its spiritual significance: in Hinduism, Lord Shiva resides at the mountain's summit. It is also where Bapu held a *Katha* (the recital of sacred texts at a religious storytelling event) in 2011; the south side of the mountain, as shown on my coat of arms, formed the backdrop to this event.

There are many more elements to a coat of arms and, of course, they probably all seem outlandish to the ordinary person. But the point of mentioning all this is that the process of designing a coat of arms for myself got me thinking about my identity and what I was actually going to do in the Lords.

The first practical task for me was finding my feet – literally, as I often got lost in the cavernous rooms and corridors of the Palace of Westminster. I had to rely on the kindness of other peers (of all parties) in finding out where to go and what to do. I always felt like I was going to embarrass myself.

And I did, of course. I was due to give my maiden speech on 24 March 2011 (the day after George Osborne's first Budget), but hadn't realised that you need to be in the chamber at the start of the debate you're speaking in. I missed that moment by seconds and my speech had to be rescheduled for 31 March, during a Labour debate on the economy that was to be opened by Labour peer and former businessman Lord Hollick.

Traditionally, maiden speeches outline the beliefs and background of the particular peer, before going on to contribute to the ongoing debate.

When my turn to speak came, I started by highlighting the importance of my guru to my life. I spoke at length about the importance of my faith, my love of Britain and my personal history of leaving Uganda – how we had left behind a prosperous past and walked towards an uncertain future, in a place unknown to us.

I paid a heartfelt tribute to the Heath government for letting me and other Ugandan Asians in. I said that this country can boast that it is one where people in genuine need of refuge can find a safe home, where they can live in peace and rebuild their lives again. And that, as if this wasn't enough, newcomers are given the same rights as those who were born in Britain, including the right to vote (a gift we particularly cherish). I said I was proud to be British and proud to be Hindu, and saw no contradiction between the two, but, on the contrary, that they reinforced each other.

I spoke next of Harrow and my parents, and of my regret that they were not here in the House to see me, before moving on to the values of enterprise that Ugandan Asians had brought with them to Britain.

This led neatly on to referencing the previous week's Budget, in which George Osborne had castigated the 'forces of stagnation' that had battered Britain's businesses during the Labour years and previously. Among these, I highlighted a tax system that is too complicated; endless employment regulations that are too costly for small businesses to implement, and that restrict job creation; a planning system recently described by Lord Wolfson as 'glacial'; and the difficulty many smaller firms had getting banks to lend them money. The latter point tied directly back to my own experience with Fast Finance, which, as I have described, was a company founded on the attempt to remedy this problem.

I welcomed the commitment of no new regulations on firms with fewer than ten staff for three years, and the simplification of the tax code.

I closed by saying that I looked forward to doing all I could to assist the government with this crucial challenge. Little did I know how true this was: within two years I found myself as the government's spokesperson in the House of Lords for the Department for Business, Innovation and Skills and the Department for Transport, a post that I would hold from January 2013 to May 2015.

I was lucky in those early days to find mentors such as Lord Dobbs, who advised me on how to act in this new and often rather confusing environment. A former political operative in Thatcher's Downing Street, Michael is now a highly successful writer (known in particular for his novel *House of Cards*, which was the inspiration for the recent Netflix drama of the same name), and it was he who convinced me that I had an obligation to write this book. Michael felt it was important that I record my perspective on becoming a Lord in my own words, particularly for the benefit of new immigrants arriving in this country.

Other important mentors in the Lords included Baroness Sharples, with whom I shared an office. She is very elegant, and would come into work every day having played golf or been swimming, even though she's over ninety. Another important figure was Lord Plumb, who was chairman of British Foods, which owned Wimpy when I worked there. I became his whip and he used to enjoy saying, 'I used to be your boss but now you're mine!' A former president of the National Farmers' Union whose father took him out of school when he was very young to run the family farm, Plumb was also a Conservative member of the European Parliament. He knows Africa well, so we bonded as a result of that, too.

Among other significant figures for me when I was still new were: Earl Attlee, whose father gave India its independence; Lord Ahmad (now a minister of state at the Foreign Office for the Commonwealth and United Nations and one of the country's highest ranking British Asian politicians); and Baroness Anelay, who was then Chief Whip (she always had a soft spot for me, acting like an older sister).

From these and other people I learned the ropes in the Lords, as well as other, more important, things about British life. My conviction deepened that freedom – economic, political and religious – is the only productive way of governing society.

I also hired my own staff as private employees within my parliamentary office, comprising a brilliant young Tory activist called Mark Fletcher, who stood against Ed Miliband in the 2015 election, and an up-and-coming young British Indian from Harrow, Ameet Jogia, who stood against the shadow secretary for trade, Barry Gardiner, in Brent North in 2017.

Both were in place by late 2011. Mark and Ameet are very different in character and outlook, but knit together like members of a regiment, imbued with common purpose and a fierce camaraderie.

During this period the two of them pretty much ran everything in my political life and I'd still be lost without them. We are three contrasting personalities, but somehow we work really well together.

Mark is very clever, with a brain the size of a melon, filled with outstanding party political and civil service knowledge. He has a rapid ability to absorb information and is utterly unafraid to speak his mind, sometimes bluntly. Mark has been the general driver of strategy and projects within my political office: he is my ideas and tactics guy. He can be ruthless beyond any of us if he feels it necessary to protect me, but is also quite emotional. Mark will tell me not just what people are thinking today, but what they will probably think tomorrow. In terms of political strategy, that is pretty invaluable.

Ameet was brought up on a council estate. When he was very young, he and his family were made homeless when they fell on hard times. He later purchased his new council property under the Right to Buy scheme, a sequence of events that would make him a great poster boy for the Tories! So much so that, as Prime Minister, David Cameron invited him to address the Conservative Party conference in 2015 to share his story. His speech, which went viral on social media in political circles, spoke of the scheme's ability to change lives: 'The Right to Buy scheme is much more than simply housing. It is about empowerment, and providing people with the opportunity to take responsibility of their own lives, and to stand on their own two feet.'

It was my son Paavan who hired Ameet for me, having ignored my objections, telling me, 'Trust me, he'll be brilliant.' And so he is. Ameet is very smooth, a natural diplomat. He is my gatekeeper and custodian of the diary; he holds me, or 'LDP' as he and Mark have dubbed me, to my schedule. He is on call 24/7, joining me in the evenings and the mornings for catch-ups and also at weekends. Ameet reminds me very much of myself as a young man (he has the same baby-faced features I had when I was his age, which people often mistake as a mark of inexperience, sometimes to their cost) – though I probably used to let my mouth run off with me more than Ameet does. He has now begun forging his own career in local politics, having been elected as a councillor in the Canons Ward of Harrow.

I think (I hope!) I have empowered Ameet and made him see what is possible, and it has certainly been a pleasure to hear his voice at the kind of public meetings in which I first began to learn about politics, and to see him begin to take the same kind of steps that I did back in the 1980s. While part of his role is to act as a conduit between me and my community, he also sometimes acts as a necessary barrier. I get a lot of requests for help and sometimes for money, and I cannot say yes to everything – and nor should I.

Both of these invaluable members of staff would stand as Conservative candidates in the 2017 general election, but their fortunes, like those of many others, suffered from inadequacies in the campaign and a sudden, last-minute surge in support for Jeremy Corbyn.

I have few rules for people I work with really closely: work comes first; there should be no blame culture; fun, in its proper place, is good; and disloyalty has no place. People working together need to look out for each other and respect each other. Of course, I have to lead. A leader needs a clear sense of purpose and vision. In whatever you are trying to achieve, you gather the best and most loyal people together and empower them with the maximum amount of delegation you can allow. Empowerment brings out the best in people and it frees up the boss to focus on the strategic matters they should be focusing on: seeing the big picture and being ahead of the game.

Without Mark and Ameet, I don't think I would have been able to see the big picture in the Lords. Effectively, we all found our feet together in Westminster. I keep these two on their toes, though, and am sometimes a bit of a slave driver, bringing over to politics the get-it-done-now philosophy that I applied in business. I am lucky that Mark, who had previously worked as assistant to an MP, is there to sometimes say to me, 'Whoa, hang on, Lord Popat, we need to think about this, and this, and this…' And I probably don't say 'no' often enough, so he helps with that. Sometimes I get Ameet to do things outside his brief because I know Mark will raise an objection, however sensible.

During Easter 2016, Mark married his long-term partner Will Knock, whom he met at university. It was a special occasion that I was honoured to share with the couple, after the Same Sex Marriage Bill which Mark had worked on was passed through Parliament.

Ameet, whom I consider an adopted son, went on to marry Priya Jatania, the daughter of a very good friend of mine for over forty years, Deepak Jatania. Deepak and I had been friends since we arrived in the UK and it was a privilege to change our friendship to one of family.

Mark and Ameet also know more about British customs than me, so I am often having to ask them, 'What do I do? What should I say? How do I act?' It's always best to ask if you don't know, I have found. Too many people cover up their lack of knowledge, and doing that causes you to make bad decisions.

The House of Lords is not my natural home – I don't belong there. The way I think about it is, 'OK, you have made it now, you are suddenly part of the establishment; it's overwhelmingly white British and public school, and you need to make sure you are not in the position of messing it up, which gives people the opportunity to say, "That chap Popat shouldn't be here."' There is still a little snobbery or coded racism in the Lords, not least of which is expressed by Labour peers, whose attitude can sometime imply, 'You brown skins should be with us.' In the corporate world, on the other hand, skills are broadly more important than skin colour.

So there is still a sense, deep inside me, that eventually I am going to be 'found out'. I am never more alert when I am in the Lords, and I don't always feel comfortable. Each time I'm in the chamber, it feels like a test.

Sometimes, wandering through the confusing corridors of the House, I feel like I am still that barefoot boy, back in Busolwe, the Ugandan village where I was born. It's insecurity, I suppose. It might be hypocritical but now and then I find myself getting Mark to sign letters or to go to meetings on my behalf, because 'Mark Fletcher' sounds so much more British than 'Dolar Popat' or 'Ameet Jogia'. I know this is wrong and that, working together, we need as a society to get beyond that sort of thinking, but the fact is, sometimes an Indian name will conjure up in someone's mind a corner-shop image. It's the other person's problem, not mine or Ameet's, but I need to get things done and if I have to utilise my aide now and then, so be it. Such strategies are part of being professional, which is very important to me.

I do think that the Lords and the British political and business establishment in general is in danger of falling behind the times in terms of how our identity politics can determine global realpolitik. We must not seem crusty or out of touch, and not assume that everyone will take the British view.

This is a serious consideration for Britain going forwards, especially post-Brexit. Entrenched attitudes could seriously affect our prosperity and standing as a nation. We Brits need to be careful about falling in love with our own pratfalls; it's often an excuse for inadequacy.

However, going beyond that serious point about Britain's habit of self-sabotage, it can often seem surreally comic, this world of high politics into which I have found myself parachuted. I'll get back into the car, after meeting a dignitary (it could be the Queen, the Prime Minister, or another head of state) and have to suppress a desire to giggle, wondering how exactly that just happened to me, the boy from Busolwe whose family couldn't afford to buy him shoes.

Both Mark and Ameet sometimes say to me that I wrongly discount those parts of my life that have helped qualify me for the role I now hold – for example, all my work in business and voluntary organisations. My rejoinder to them is that every new role represents a learning curve and that I need to learn how to be a Lord, just as I had to learn how to be a waiter at the Wimpy bar, someone managing a sub-post office, a financier of small businesses or someone running a group of care homes and hotels. Sometimes, too, despite all my hard work, it seems to me like my success in business and then joining the Lords happened organically – that I was lucky and can't claim that much credit for it.

I am someone who hates to make excuses, but early on I explained to Mark and Ameet about my past: my Ugandan background and the feelings of exclusion and shame I experienced there as a youngster, beginning with the lucky dip incident. They understood. Ameet's own family were originally from Tanzania (where he still has relatives), while Mark had some experience of being treated like an outsider as a gay man who grew up in Doncaster.

On that note, there used to be a lot of reticence regarding LGBT issues in the British Indian community, often as a result of not only ignorance but also parental expectations about the route their children should take in life. However, the community is opening up and now British Asian LGBT weddings are becoming increasingly common occurrences.

There is no such thing as a typical day for me in the Lords, but there are broad parameters. I will tend to get up about 5.30 a.m., go through my emails and do my research for the day (often to prepare for a speech). Then I will make a cup of tea and go back to bed with a newspaper, usually *The Times*. I love *The Times*, which I read every day without fail, getting it delivered at home even when I am away so I can catch up when I get back. Mark complains that I will pick up a story from three weeks ago and say, 'Why didn't we do anything on this?' Before ten-thirty I will usually speak to both Mark and Ameet for about five minutes each. Then I sometimes go for a walk or go to the gym (like many British Indians, I am in danger of developing diabetes and need to watch my blood sugar levels).

Normally at 12.30 p.m., I drive myself or Ameet picks me up and we head off to the Lords, while I phone Mark again to ask him to get specific things done as they have occurred to me over the past couple of hours – at least three, usually more. Generally it's something like, 'We need to write to so-and-so,' and I'll usually expect it done by the time I get into the House. More recently, I have been taking the Underground, Stanmore to Westminster: forty-five minutes door to door. By the time I get home in the evening, it's normally 10 p.m.

I am quite impatient, I am afraid to say, and my aides have learned to interpret a single word as an instruction to carry out a whole chain of actions. Mark once joked, 'Lord Popat, you ask me how I am every morning and never stop to listen. I could say, "I lost my leg last night" and I don't think you'd notice.' I like it that Mark feels able to make such cracks at me, but fear I will not ever cure my impatient nature. I try to respond to everything within forty-eight hours, though obviously that is not always possible; sometimes, in business as in politics, one has to wait for the right moment.

In 2012, as Conservative Party chairman, Andrew Feldman asked me to develop a new venture called the Conservative Friends of India (CF India). This was an alliance between the Conservative Party, Indian parliamentarians and companies, and British Indians in general. The idea was to develop both links and a meaningful dialogue between Indian politicians, businesses and professional groups, and their counterparts in Britain. CF India was modelled on Conservative Friends of Israel (CFI) – a very effective political organisation. It was the first time anyone had tried to marry up the political and business interests of leading Indians and British Indians, whose communities together represent a market of around 1.2 billion potential customers. So CF India was a smart move.

As founding chairman, it took an awful lot of my time to get CF India up and running, but all that work felt worth it when, at the group's launch in 2012 at the Royal Horticultural Halls near Westminster, I watched David Cameron address the 1,200-strong audience and offer people the vision that a British Indian Tory might one day be Prime Minister. As he put it, 'The great thing about the Conservative Party is that we might be a bit crusty, we might be a bit old fashioned, but we often make the big breakthroughs.' As evidence of this, he cited the example of the Tories having the first Jewish Prime Minister, Benjamin Disraeli, and the first female Prime Minister, Margaret Thatcher.

The emphasis here was that the launch was unprecedented – and 'long overdue', as I put it in my introductory speech. It was, in fact, the largest political gathering of British Indians in recent times and would remain so until a visit to the UK by Indian Prime Minister Narendra Modi in November 2015 where he addressed British Indians at Wembley Stadium. Labour were, I think, quite threatened by this new movement.

At this landmark political occasion, Cameron also paid tribute to British Indians and east African British Indians in particular. He mentioned that Indian businesses own some of the most iconic British brands, such as Jaguar Land Rover. We invited Narendra Modi, who at that stage was still Chief Minister of Gujarat.

In March of that year, I had written to Modi explaining my view that India is central to the new world order, adding that I felt it was in Britain's best interest to strengthen the ties between our two nations. He agreed to come, but then ended up being pressed for time, sending in his place Smriti Irani, then a Gujarati MP and later a prominent Cabinet minister who was to hold a number of different departmental briefs.

David Cameron's visit to the Neasden Temple in 2013 was another big deal. Both this and the launch of the Conservative Friends of India certainly helped Cameron and the Conservative Party to victory in 2015. (The video to 'Neela hai Asman', a Hindi song commissioned by CF India that encouraged voters to back David Cameron, also played its part, going viral internationally in the weeks leading up to the election.) Working hard on these and other projects also constituted a big shift for Mark and Ameet, as it brought them into contact with a much wider array of people in political life.

The events at Westminster and then Neasden also gave a sense of belonging to those who attended, as well as the sense that we were no longer immigrants but part of the social fabric. In his speech at the Royal Horticultural Halls, Cameron said that the Ugandan Asians were 'possibly the most successful group of immigrants anywhere at any point in history'. No British Prime Minister had ever spoken so highly of our community.

10

BECOMING A MINISTER

I stood down as chairman of the Conservative Friends of India after my appointment as a government Lord in Waiting and a Conservative whip in January 2013. The invitation to take on this new role (which required me to stand down from involvement in any business) was issued while I was in Thailand; Mark sent me a text saying, 'You have been made a minister, according to the Downing Street website!' As with the original invitation to join the Lords, it took me a bit of time to catch up!

That night, I had had dinner in a restaurant in Bangkok, and left my phone behind. I went back to get it and there was a text asking me to ring Lord Hill, who had just been appointed as the Leader of the House of Lords. But by then it was 4.30 a.m. in London. I phoned Jonathan back the next day, but by then he was at Balmoral, to have an audience with the Queen. The reception was poor up in Scotland when I rang, so we couldn't hear each other. I texted him instead, saying, 'It was a privilege to serve.'

That text changed my life. I cannot stress my gratitude at having been given such a privilege. However, this new role represented a significant step up for me. As a businessman during the Labour period, I had been very critical of the role of government: 'Get off our backs, cut red tape, deregulate, lower taxes, more support for SMEs, more exports' – that was always my line. I liked to make a joke first made, I think, by Ronald Reagan: 'If it moves, tax it. If it keeps moving, regulate it. And if it stops moving, subsidise it.' Or to quip, 'I've come from government and I am here to help.'

But now here I was, in government, getting involved in the nitty-gritty of taxation, regulation and subsidy.

After I got the news of my appointment, I was flying home via Ahmedabad, where I was due to meet Narendra Modi (then still the Chief Minister of Gujarat), along with our High Commissioner to India, James Bevan. At the time, I was busy with a campaign to reinstate formal relations between Britain and Gujarat. This meeting represented the beginning of engaging with – but not en-dorsing – Modi. Due to my new government appointment, I could no longer attend the meeting, as Modi meeting a British minister would be seen as an official endorsement (this is the Foreign Office's protocol, about which I shall say nothing more!). Instead, I went to see my guru Morari Bapu in Mumbai for his blessings for my appointment. He approved, but also offered me some wise words about conducting politics on the basis of common nationality, not exclusive community.

To explain, being a government whip and a Lord in Waiting is a ministerial position in the government, but it is also linked to the Royal Household through historic precedent (so in official terms I was a member of the Royal Household). In the House of Com-mons, the job of the whips is to manage the business of the House and, above all, to make sure there are enough MPs to support the passage of legislation. In the Lords it is slightly different, as the whips also have to represent the government from the despatch box, as ministers do in the Commons. My responsibility was to act as spokesperson for two departments: the Department for Business, Innovation and Skills and the Department for Transport, responding to questions, participating in debates and helping to pass legislation.

I found my duties as a whip both intriguing and exhausting. Whips are like secret policeman, and there are times when they don't enjoy a great reputation. They can be pushy with their flocks but there are moments when they must show compassion, according to circumstances. The whip's main job is to make sure people from their party are there to vote. They also collect intelligence. The current Speaker of the House of Commons, John Bercow, recently observed that the House of Commons needs whips in the same way that any other house needs sewers. But whips are very important in the communication process between backbenchers, the Lords and party leadership, with information flowing between individuals, the Chief Whip's Office (the engine room of the process) and the Cabinet or shadow Cabinet, as the case may be.

The whip's role includes counting numbers, ensuring attendance and, above all, winning votes. It is all about persuasion, ensuring policies in a manifesto can be implemented. At the same time, there is a pastoral role, which involves making sure Lords and MPs are getting on OK in their day-to-day duties, and life in general.

Whips meet for thirty minutes on afternoons on the days the Lords is sitting to discuss any important government business and strategy. On Wednesdays, we would meet early for an hour, the deputy whip from the Commons coming in to brief the whips in the Lords.

The Lord in Waiting aspect of being a whip in the Lords involves representing the royals on different occasions. For example, when President Sata of Zambia passed away during a state visit to Britain, I was part of the official process to repatriate his body. Although the roles of Lord in Waiting and whip are linked, the responsibilities they carry are separate. This meant I also ended up going to President Sata's funeral in Zambia, but this time as a representative of the government, flying out to Lusaka with Sophie, Countess of Wessex, who was representing the Queen.

Then there is the ministerial role, which is the big difference between being a government whip in the Commons and a government whip in the Lords. As a Minister of the Crown representing both the Department of Business, Innovation and Skills and the Department of Transport, I had to answer questions at the despatch box on behalf of the government. Usually there were clear lines to take, based on established Conservative policy, but often, too, I would have to sit down with Mark and Ameet and work out what to say.

It's quite nerve-racking, having to speak at the despatch box in the Lords, and there is absolutely no training. You are simply thrown in at the deep end. Sometimes it would involve slimming down a forty-page civil service briefing into just a couple of sides of A4. That's a big responsibility as you are inevitably editing for salience as well as length, and you are always speaking on behalf of the government not yourself, despite the fact it is you who is doing the editing. Mark and Ameet really helped with this, despite running into occasional problems in that the civil service will only deal directly with the principal person involved in the editing process, (i.e. me). Mark and Ameet would watch me from the gallery and we'd have a debrief immediately afterwards, with them pointing out where I had done well and where I had stumbled.

Sometimes the questions I'd get were quite hard to answer, and now and then I got ripped up by my Labour opposite number. Once I made an error to do with the fateful question of whether we would be leaving the EU and got hauled in by the Chief Whip. Another time, acting in my own capacity as a whip, I let a debate go on longer than it should have.

But there have been good moments, too, like getting one over Lord Sugar (no mean feat) on a question to do with the Royal Mail. One odd thing is how you find yourself becoming an expert in arcane areas, one for me being cycling safety.

Debates are much easier than answering questions from the despatch box as you are reading off a prepared script that you have had time to draft and think about, even if you do deviate while giving the speech in order to take into account what has been said by the previous speakers. The worst thing is when another minister is away and you have to answer questions on something way out of your comfort zone. I once had to deal with questions about the safety and security of drones because the defence minister was away. (It was reckoned that because drones move, they could feasibly come under 'transport' and thus I was the correct second choice!)

As parliamentary legislation proceeds, whether it relates to transport or anything else, there is much frank and open discussion between party and government whips in the Lords, and also across the two Houses. However, it was more difficult getting things done when we were in coalition with the Lib Dems, as there were many issues that the coalition partners came to from very different starting points – plus, there were a lot of Lib Dem peers in the Lords (too many, probably).

Of course, the power-sharing arrangement changed with the

May 2015 election, when David Cameron and the Conservative Party won an outright majority. I was very proud and happy when this happened. Cameron was the first Prime Minister since the turn of the new century to continue in office with a larger share of the vote following a term of more than five years, and the only Prime Minister other than Margaret Thatcher to continue in office immediately after a term of at least four years with a greater number of seats. Those are pretty impressive statistics.

The key thing for me was that the trend established in 2010 for increasing support for the Conservatives among the British Indian community had strengthened. In the 2015 election, British Indian support for Labour dwindled amid a general collapse in Labour's ethnic vote.

After the party's assertive success in May, Cameron responded by immediately integrating ethnic minority politicians into his new Cabinet, for example appointing Priti Patel as Minister for Employment. The new crop of MPs included Rishi Sunak, elected as Member for Richmond. Similarly, in council elections we saw a rise in British Indian Conservative councillors, such as my assistant Ameet Jogia, Meenal Sachdev, Mina Parmar, Abhishek Sachdev, Hiten Ganatra , Reena Ranger OBE and many others.

However, it was time for me to move on from my ministerial post and I stood down in the same month as the general election, but continued on as a party whip. I must admit, I was quite relieved to stand down – being a minister is a bit like doing exams, every working day!

I am lucky in that in my continuing role as a whip I report to John Taylor, the Chief Whip of the House of Lords. He is the best boss I've had and I get on with him very well. Chief Whip is one of the toughest jobs in the Lords. I admire John's passion and resilience – the past few years have been incredibly challenging.

My next big role in government was that of Prime Minister's trade envoy to Uganda and Rwanda. I took up this position in January 2016 and am still in post as I write.

I also became vice chair of the All-Party Parliamentary Group for the Commonwealth. The purpose of this body is: to inform MPs about the Commonwealth Secretariat's efforts to strengthen the Commonwealth network; to keep members aware of the range of non-parliamentary activities and programmes carried out underneath the Commonwealth brand, both on governmental and non-governmental levels; and to take advantage of opportunities within the developing Commonwealth network for Britain's political and commercial activities, and for Britain's positioning in the new international landscape.

Along with my good friend Andrew Mitchell, the former Secretary of State for International Development, I started another All-Party Parliamentary Group in 2018 for Rwanda. One of our aims was to continue strengthening links with Africa and to dispel negative misconceptions of the continent. We successfully campaigned for the Commonwealth Heads of Government Meeting, a biennial summit meeting of the heads of government from all Commonwealth nations, to be held in Rwanda in 2020.

The African envoyship to both Rwanda and Uganda is a position in which I feel that all my skills really come together. I consider it an honour to sit in the mother of all parliaments every day, but I am well aware that my position comes with responsibilities. I am determined to make sure I work hard to support trade between Britain, Uganda and Rwanda, and across the Commonwealth more generally.

Now, when I meet with one of the two respective heads of state, President Museveni of Uganda or President Kagame of Rwanda, I am sure of my political remit as never before. The envoyship marries my love of east Africa, my entrepreneurial spirit and my knowledge of business and finance, as well as my desire to get things done quickly: in ninety-minute meetings with Museveni and Kagame, I think I have been able to cover matters that would normally take the government six months to build up to discussing. I am very proud of this. It feels as if my complex national and cultural identity perfectly equips me to make the most of this opportunity at this particular point in time.

11

FLOWS OF IDENTITY

From time to time one needs to step back and examine the question of identity in all its complex detail.

My primary identity is British. As I have explained, I believe in that wholeheartedly. When I think today about my life and how genuinely incredible it is – a gorgeous, kind, brilliant partner in Sandhya, the financial security that I dreamed about as a child, great friends and exciting new experiences all the time – I feel overwhelming appreciation for the United Kingdom. The UK is my second god. I know that sounds corny, but it's the way I feel.

My wife Sandhya has been at the heart of the family part of my identity: the woman I love and my best friend. Since the beginning of our relationship in 1980, Sandhya has played a devoted role in supporting me – first in business and then in politics. I am always acutely aware that she sacrificed her career for mine, giving up her job at Glaxo.

My three sons have also supported me and given my life meaning. Of course, it's not for me to pass judgement on what kind of parent I have been to our children, but I feel Sandhya and I did our best, and now we have the great joy of being close to all of them. Our family has recently grown again after the marriage of my eldest son

Rupeen. Our loving daughter-in-law Rupa is a wonderful addition to the family and what makes it even more special is that she is the daughter of the Ganatras – a family I have known since I came to the UK and who were among the first friends I made here.

The next part of my identity is religion. I think that religion is a lifeline for human beings – it gives us meaning and purpose. But religion cannot change the nationality of a person, nor can it dry up the ancestral blood in one's veins. Hindus believe on many different levels and with different shades of intensity, and in my youth and early manhood I was a fairly ordinary kind of Hindu.

I have described meeting Yogiji Maharaj at the age of fourteen, an encounter that probably helped keep me more on track than I might otherwise have been. But it is Morari Bapu, my guru, who has made the real difference to my religious identity. He has kept me balanced on the tightrope of life; indeed, his teachings have *become* my life. If Yogiji Maharaj was primary school, Morari Bapu was secondary.

There are very few people of whom you can say, 'They changed my life,' and I began wanting to enable others to experience this. In 1999, I sponsored a *Katha* (or recital of sacred texts) by Bapu at Wembley Arena, which was attended by 65,000 people over nine days. Each in different phases of life, all of the attendees were seeking spiritual guidance and solace.

Bapu stayed with Sandhya and I at home during this *Katha*. My experience of these nine days at Wembley shaped my future, giving my life a new meaning and purposeful course.

I am not sure what Bapu thought about the invitation for him to stay with us. I later learned that he had been briefed that I wasn't a truly spiritual man, that I hung around with politicians and let alcohol be consumed in my house. It was true that I used to have a rather fine Scottish-style bar at home which I used to entertain business clients. Bapu did come to stay with us in Stanmore, although he wasn't sure what to expect when he arrived, and I myself was certainly very unsure of the protocols involved in having him as a guest. The house had been cleaned and he was staying in my and Sandhya's room, but I wasn't sure if we should remove the picture of Bapu from the bedroom.

'Why do you need that? I'm here myself!' Bapu responded, in perplexity.

Both before and during the *Katha*, Bapu would be by the fireplace in the garden patio every morning, praying. One day, not knowing any better, I wandered through the garden in my swimming costume and dove into the pool. Then the next day I set off jogging.

I think Bapu came to see that I wasn't a bad man, but rather a man who was somewhat lacking in knowledge of the details of spiritual observance. It was, anyway, a fairly frenetic period: over fifty people would arrive on our doorstep every morning to try to gain an audience with Bapu, and this stream required constant management.

During the nine days of the *Katha* at Wembley, my two older sons, Rupeen (then sixteen) and Paavan (then fourteen), managed nearly everything on my behalf (they had just finished their exams). I was happy to delegate and just let them get on with it, each of them walking round the venue armed with a walkie-talkie. Effectively, Rupeen and Paavan ran the whole event. It is pretty amazing, in my view, what the boys accomplished.

It's important to be able to delegate and empower. On the first day we didn't have enough food and no one was sure what to do.

Paavan coolly got on the phone and ordered a rice dish for 1,000 people; I was very proud. (The company in question was Meera Catering, which my family – and Bapu – still use and which has since grown into a massive business.)

I have since been on many retreats and attended many *Kathas* with Bapu, ranging from small, intimate gatherings of his followers to enormous recitals in London, Rome and Athens. In August 2011, I joined a group of Bapu's followers for a nine-day reading of Hindu sacred texts on Mount Kailash (which went on to feature on my coat of arms). Kailash sits in the mountains of Tibet known as the 'roof of the world'. It was an honour to be in such a spiritual place, where the air is thin, but you can feel closer to God.

Bapu became my mentor and guide. Any good that I have done, he has inspired it. Whatever my manifold faults, he made me a better person for knowing him: stronger; more loyal; more confident; more thankful for what I have; more hopeful about life's possibilities and more joyful in fulfilling them; quicker to share jokes and humour; and more courageous in accepting my limitations.

After building this connection with Bapu, Hinduism stopped being 'just' my religion and became instead a way of life. He stamped thoughts of my religion into my everyday practice. His Hinduism was muscular, not limp or restrictive. He was a thinker, not a preacher. His thoughts were bold, ground-breaking and – for a Hindu living in a Christian country – visionary. Bapu's liberalism attracted me to listen to him and whenever possible visit him. I think of him as a spiritual and not a religious leader (actually, he does not like being called a 'leader' at all).

I have never met a greater man than Bapu. I feel him with me as I write now. I feel him beside me always. Having listened to him for the past twenty years, I find in his teachings and influence an insistent reminder that life has to be lived for a purpose. He has encouraged me in the idea that my whole purpose is to engage British Indians in the political life of this country, starting with a grass-roots sense of duty to the community and the country as a whole.

Bapu also enabled me to see that part of my role should involve educating the Conservative Party, to help it learn about British Indians and about how so many of us share its values; and, just as important, to stop the party on its occasional wrong turns into narrowness and solipsism.

Someone else who has been a mentor for my work to widen the community's political engagement was Manubhai Madhvani, one of the great gentlemen of the Gujarati diaspora. In many ways, during his exile Manubhai was the leader in Britain of the Ugandan Asian community thrown out by Amin, as well of both the *Lohana* community and Hindus more generally. (Manubhai tells his story in his own book, *Tide of Fortune.*) Since the Madhvanis' expulsion and later triumphant return to Uganda, where their business is again a leading force in the economy, I have become very friendly with the family.

I am particularly grateful to Manubhai, as it was he who first encouraged me to go into public life, many years ago. He was great at understanding people, someone who always took time to listen. Manubhai passed away in 2011; I deeply miss his guidance.

While the religious dimension of my identity is crucially important to me, this does not mean I believe Hinduism should become a minor state religion of Britain. On the contrary, Britain is a Christian country and we should be proud of it as such. During 2015, I remember a lot of nonsense was talked about the de-Christianisation of Britain. A cinema chain made the news for banning a sixty-second advert that featured the Lord's Prayer. They feared the advert, produced by the Church of England, would offend. Then a major report written by Baroness Butler-Sloss declared Britain to no longer be a Christian country. This assessment was supported by a number of bodies, including those in the Asian community. The House of Lords came under particular criticism, given its members were overly representative of the Church of England.

The rationale behind these arguments against state religion faces two major obstacles. The first is that many of the people practising non-Christian religions in Britain came here because it's a Christian country in which religious tolerance is prized. There are depressingly few countries where freedom of speech and the right to religious practice are upheld as they are here, and Christianity is the religion that underpins that double freedom. As a Hindu, I truly value the moral and ethical framework that Christianity provides. It angers me that this enabling framework should itself become subject to the same kind of intolerance that religious groups of many types suffer in other countries.

My second objection to the de-Christianisation of Britain is that while the numbers of churchgoers might have declined, Britain remains an overwhelmingly Christian country in cultural terms. Rather than trying to undermine this – whether through institutional erosion, calls for state secularism in the media, or the much, much worse scourge of religion-inflected violence of the type practised by ISIS and other fundamentalist groups – we should be celebrating Britain's religious heritage alongside our own. Hindus in particular should be looking for commonalities between the Hindu and Christian faiths.

Encouraging active dialogue between religions is important to me. In 2011 I gave a speech at the launch of the British Hindu–Christian forum in London, an event that formed part of that year's Inter Faith Week. I began by saying that my own personal Hindu–Christian dialogue started forty-five years ago and 4,000 miles away in Uganda: I was born a Hindu but went to a Christian school, and so developed an early interest in the parallels between our faiths. In Uganda, we would happily celebrate Christmas *and* Eid (a habit from childhood I've been happy to keep up since), and people of different faiths lived happily side by side.

I continued by describing all religions being like different pathways – each with their own individual character, but all leading to the same summit. A wise man once likened these journeys to a passage up a mountain. God is the pinnacle looking down on all those travellers walking towards him. However, each of the travellers can only see those companions that are travelling with them on the same path. It is only when they reach the top that they can look down and realise that there are people coming up from all sides of the mountain. This is exactly what Inter Faith Week is all about: the realisation and acknowledgement that there are so many different faiths all reaching for the same goals of peace, prosperity and happiness. We are all climbing the same mountain. Promoting this message of unity between faiths, of mutual respect and understanding, is an essential one for the difficult times that we live in.

I have been pleasantly surprised at the number of times faith has been debated and discussed in the House of Lords. During a debate on multiculturalism, the then Chief Rabbi, Lord Sacks, made an important point. He said that religion is undoubtedly a good thing: it creates communities and teaches people to make sacrifices for the sake of others. The bad news, Lord Sacks went on, is that every community also divides as it unites, because for every 'us' there is a 'them'.

It is through inter-faith dialogue that we can address this challenge. In our daily lives, we also need to allow other religions to affect us and not be self-centred in our approach, focusing on commonalities rather than differences. Paramahansa Yogananda (1893–1952), an Indian yogi and guru who introduced millions of Indians and Westerners to the teachings of meditation and yoga, once said, 'When you are dancing with the waves of the ocean, you can't get a perspective of the ocean as a whole, but from the air you have a bird's-eye view of its vast expanse.' It's only looking from above and breaking away from our self-centredness that we can truly appreciate and acknowledge the parallels between different faiths.

I see this principle in action in the House of Lords. Every day before business begins, we have Christian prayers delivered by one of the bishops in the House. Even though I'm a Hindu, I've always found these prayers to be energising and a stark reminder that we're here to represent something bigger than our respective political parties and ourselves.

As well as my political party, nationality, family and religion, my identity runs even deeper – as a British Indian, a British Gujarati and, to granulate further, a British *Lohana*. The *Lohana* community in London is a hive of social activity and I'm very proud of the successes the community has had, and how willing so many of its members have been to support worthwhile projects for all the population.

The positive actions of the *Lohanas* are one reason I and the great majority of British Indians were against moves to introduce a caste discrimination amendment to the Equality Act 2010. I've never known the British Indian community be so opposed to a change in the law. This resistance brought together different organisations, in the Hindu community in particular, which have never worked together before.

Discrimination on the grounds of 'caste' is something that has rightly been left behind and to try to make it a factor in legislation being passed in 21st-century Britain seems utterly outrageous, and runs the risk of stopping ethnic groups doing some really good work. It is a mistake to rush through an amendment to the law that would stigmatise and insult the Hindu community (which is inclusive and open to reform). Anyway, I oppose the idea that our society is riddled with caste prejudice. All political parties need to appreciate the sensitivities behind this issue and not accuse British Hindus of discriminatory practices where they actually don't exist.

That said, as a community, *Lohanas* currently stand at a crossroads. We need to be more open to marriage beyond our group. We need to erase our generational differences, and bridge the gap between our experienced elders and the youth who are our future. Previously, our priority was our children, but that focus must now widen. Our older generation now have pressing needs: the government can't provide for all of them, so the community needs to work together on this to deliver solutions.

A lot of *Lohana* customs are still very outdated, such as inviting hundreds of people to weddings, funeral arrangements going on for weeks, and so on. In these respects, our community needs reform and we should work together to evolve, especially as many of our members can do so without the unnecessary financial pressures of funding complex ceremonies. Another thing we need to do is encourage more cultural activity, as many of our stories and tales are in danger of being forgotten.

The need for immigrant communities to be less insular extends to other activities and ways we can look to integrate. In terms of charity work and philanthropy, for example, both Hindus and Muslims alike need to volunteer a bit more to help those outside their own communities. How frequently do you meet a young British Indian who is a trustee of a non-Indian charity?

This is not to say that British Indians do not volunteer or help the community. Far from it. I know so many people who do their bit. Yet, so often, we find British Indians working in or raising money for organisations primarily aimed at their own communities. It is time we break down these barriers and take this important step further forwards.

It is vital that we use our broadest possible definition of charity and do not limit ourselves by race, religion or creed. Through supporting a hospice, for example, we can promote inter-faith dialogue, tolerance and understanding, as well as contribute to the community – all in one go.

I can hear people saying, 'Well have you put your money where your mouth is?' Yes, I have. I have been involved with a number of Indian community organisations, as well as being a founding director of St Luke's Hospice. It is our local hospice in Harrow, which I helped establish in 1987. It is an asset to our local community and a place for which I have a huge soft spot. I am now its chief patron, and feel that starting the hospice may perhaps be one of my greatest legacies. I am proud to host an annual event for St Luke's in the House of Lords to thank all the volunteers for their selfless service to mankind.

Back in the 1990s there was no hospice or care for members of the Asian community, unlike the special Jewish hospices that existed then. Today, St Luke's is well accustomed to caring for the large Asian population in Brent and Harrow. All the care the centre provides is absolutely free.

I hosted the twenty-fifth and thirtieth anniversary celebrations in the Lords, with guest speaker Lord Howard, who is chairman of Hospice UK. It was also an honour to host a special reception at 10 Downing Street with Samantha Cameron to thank the volunteers, supporters and donors of the hospice for the excellent work they do.

I have also been an advisor to Nightingale Hammerson, which offers care facilities for Jewish people. In addition, I fund my own registered charity, The Lord Dolar Popat Foundation, which makes contributions to medical and educational institutions. And in the past five years, I have made contributions in excess of £1 million to charities and voluntary organisations. Sandhya's own charity, The Lady Popat Foundation, is similarly active and has made contributions of a similar volume.

I offer these as examples of practice to other British Indians, not as boasts. The practice of philanthropy needs constant vigilance. Speaking generally, we British Indians need to be more transparent about our own charities. Sadly, too many British Indian charities are still not forthcoming about their funding and organisation. Thousands of British Indians support good causes, but the question we too rarely ask ourselves is, 'Do we know where that money goes?'

We live in the age of the internet; it is no longer acceptable for British Indian organisations not to openly publish accounts and information on elections and nominations. There needs to be accountability. Similarly, we have a generation of British-born youngsters who have benefited from the incredible education this country offers. We need to invite them into the fold and to bring in fresh ideas; they are our future and we should empower them. We should say, 'Your generation is rewriting the rulebook every day; you aren't limited to the family business or being a doctor or lawyer; you can do whatever you want!'

We need to get away from inwardness both ethnically and generationally. In 2012, I was invited by City Hindus Network – a network of over 3,000 highly educated Hindus working in the City of London – to give a speech. It was their annual Diwali dinner and I was their chief guest and keynote speaker. Instead of wishing them Happy Diwali, I decided on a frontal assault.

'Many of you will think of me as an admirer of the Muslim community,' I began. And as I paused for effect, I sensed an expectation among my audience that I would then go on to say, 'But…' Instead, I simply said, 'And so I am.'

The tension was broken at once. 'Yes, I do admire them,' I continued, 'as they are willing to do civic duty as school governors, judges, councillors, MPs etc.' I went on to say that I believe my own Hindu community just isn't doing enough. It's staying inward in many aspects of British nationhood except business. There are gaps in social leadership, gaps in awareness and family constraints that stop bright Hindus coming forward and taking a full role in civic life. Too often, in my view, we British Hindus retreat into our business and professional bastions and don't get involved in the civic process.

An important part of political responsibility with respect to questions of identity is preventing the radicalisation of young people through the twisting of their faith into something perverse and dangerous. Young people need to be taught what is true and what is not true about their own religions, and those in civic life need to take a role in this process.

This has, as is well known, been a particular problem for the Muslim community. This is quite strange, given that by and large Muslims are more active in British political and public life than the members of any other faith besides Jews and Christians.

But this is not just a matter for one community or another. All these questions need to be seen in the context of the larger picture of immigration into Britain. Britain has been a magnet to citizens throughout the world for the past two hundred years; from the Jews of Germany to the builders of Ireland to the nurses of the Caribbean; from the businessmen of India and America to the plumbers of Eastern Europe. Brexit or no Brexit, it is a fact that our language, culture, freedom and opportunities have continued to entice those who are looking for a new home.

This is not unproblematic. When I first came to Britain in 1971 there were the Scots, the Irish, the Indians, Pakistanis and the Afro-Caribbeans here. Now we have a large number of people from different parts of Africa and Eastern Europe. The degree of diversity in Britain has changed dramatically, and the more diverse the society, the less likely its citizens are to share common values.

Immigration is a very important issue for ordinary people. Since the expansion of membership of the European Union, there have been more Eastern Europeans coming to the UK than expected. While numbers have fallen in the face of Brexit, this still puts tremendous pressure on the NHS, and on education and social services. On the other hand, Britain needs migrants to fulfil our skills shortage. In my opinion there needs to be selective immigration here as there is in Australia.

The influence of immigration has been felt everywhere in Britain, for good and bad. Some communities have found it easier than others: the Jews, the Hindus, the Sikhs and a large part of the Muslim community are fully integrated into British life and share the values that underpin this great country. It is to be celebrated that we can now give back to a country that has given us so much.

But there are also people in some communities, often children and younger people, who have been born and raised here but feel completely alienated from life in Britain. The children of first-generation immigrants sometimes feel more divorced from life in Britain than their parents. A tiny minority of these will go on to use terrorism to redress their alienation. A simple first step is that everyone should be fluent in English. Learning the native language brings the social skills that are the bedrock of integration.

We must also use education in order to cut the growth of alienation at its root – this is a job for parents, for schools, for politicians, the media and for society in general. As a whole, those with immigrant heritage should not forget how far we have come: integrating into British society, adopting British values and cherishing great British institutions like Parliament and the monarchy. We must also remember how far Britain has come: how it has embraced so many diverse populations, religions and cultures (not always without trouble or resentment) and managed to retain its charm, openness and character.

Yet there are still people living in Britain who preach against its values, who promote separation and isolation and who seek to pressurise the state into treating immigrants differently to everybody else. This is wrong. It is not and should not be the British way to allow a state-sponsored situation to unfold in which one community or religion lives in complete isolation to another.

Of course we should respect diverse cultures and acknowledge our differences, but we shouldn't encourage people to live apart or to reject basic British values. As the former Chief Rabbi put it, some types of multiculturalism enable people to use Britain as a kind of hotel whereby 'guests' who pay their taxes are given private spaces, so separate cultures can live behind locked doors, merely being serviced by the 'hotel management' (in this case the state) without having a sense of belonging or feeling any responsibility to the society or the country they live in. I believe that state-sponsored multiculturalism (as differentiated from the multiculturalism that happens organically) can easily become a wrong-headed doctrine. It can foster difference between communities and it can stop us from strengthening our collective identity. Indeed, it can deliberately weaken it.

This type of multiculturalism in many ways hands victory to our enemies: to those who want to divide us and those who oppose British values. Longer-term, doctrinal multiculturalism will not strengthen society – it will undermine it. A lot more work is needed on encouraging integration so that we can all contribute to society and live in it side by side. We should encourage politicians to enhance cohesion and build a stronger society rather than putting more difference into the system and sanctioning it. We must have a level playing field, where we respect differences but ultimately focus on common ground.

Ethnic identity in Britain has been manipulated to entrench the right to difference, which is a divisive concept. What we need is the right to equal treatment despite difference: that's a unifying concept and is what's at the heart of what I mean whenever I write 'we' in the context of being British.

We do not want people to feel that because they are different they can do exactly what they want and follow their own laws. What we need to do is say, 'Yes, you are different and that is OK, you will be given equal treatment and we will respect your right to be different, but you must obey the laws of Britain and be part of the whole.'

That is why I have significant concerns about faith schools. It seems absolutely daft to ghettoise children. Even if that's not the intention, we're effectively creating apartheid in education. The world we live in now is plural; people of every different race, gender and religion have to be able to empathise with one another and coexist. My fear is that faith schools promote the opposite of that principle; effectively, they encourage people of the same faiths to congregate together rather than to seek out – and learn from – people of other cultures. Many of the areas in the UK, if not the world, that suffer the worst community tensions are those in which people of different faiths and backgrounds are poorly integrated, and where each community sticks together, with very little overlap.

I believe it is wrong for Hindu schools – or for that matter, schools of any faith – to deny the value of the experiences our children gain in interacting with people from different backgrounds. We wouldn't expect people to be segregated by religion in the workplace – indeed it is illegal to do so in the UK – and I think we have to be very careful about allowing it in education. Where faith schools are allowed, then it is incumbent on them to ensure they work incredibly hard to overcome the narrow-mindedness and inward-looking approach that can result if a community only speaks to itself. I believe that if we are to have faith schools, then 50 per cent of their pupils should come from faiths other than the one that gives the school its official identity.

I think it is vital that governors of faith schools ensure that other faiths are taught, and that the extent to which they are taking this commitment seriously is monitored. We owe it to our children to ensure they are as prepared as possible to understand the world around them, and schools play a big part in developing that understanding.

So, I am proud to be a Hindu, but I am also very conscious that it is British culture and its championing of religious freedom that makes this possible. Many of the speeches I have given and the articles I have written crystallise around this idea of coherent freedom.

The British establishment still has a great duty to make 'freedom' feel real for immigrants. As David Cameron cogently put it during his speech at one of Bapu's *Kathas* at Wembley, 'In the past, we thought it was enough to remove formal barriers to entry and to provide equality of opportunity. But it wasn't … An open door is not the same as an *invitation* to come in.'

At the same time, it is not the British way to allow extreme multiculturalism, where one community or religion lives in complete isolation to another. Those that are aggressively looking to promote difference and thus undermine community cohesion must be challenged and stopped, not only because this contrasts positive British values, but also because it is dangerous.

Extreme multiculturalism does not strengthen society, it undermines it. In Britain, there is so much more that unites than divides us; there are so many elements of our national identity that we should champion and be proud of – elements that people around the world are still fighting and dying for today. The bedrock of these elements is freedom, in particular the freedom to vote and the freedom to practise one's religion.

As immigrants, the politics of the previous generation may have placed our ethnicity front and centre, and rightly so, but we are now all British citizens, so our focus must be different. Further, politics is no longer so colour- or class-driven as it once was. We are fine with diversity, and we must foster solidarity. We should adopt statements such as, 'Proud to be British and proud to be Hindu,' or 'Proud to be British and proud to be Muslim,' and we should feel lucky that we have the chance to make them.

That said, we must continue to be forthright going forwards. Below the surface, a series of questions about British identity remain. Issues relating to race, immigration and national identity always rise to the surface in difficult times, but we must face the challenge and show that organisations like the British National Party and the National Front are wrong. Such groups must not have a monopoly over phrases like 'Proud to be British' and use them to justify divisive tactics.

Part of this move to promote a more flexible sense of what it means to be British involves each of the organisations that represent different religions speaking to the media and the state with one voice. We tend to forget that the government can provide leadership, but only people and communities can deliver change. Therefore, for our democratic process to function properly, we need each of our religious communities to come together and agree what the government needs to hear from them.

Faiths other than Hinduism offer good models for faith-based approaches to government. The Board of Jewish Deputies represents the whole Jewish community as a united voice when representing Jewish interests to the British government; and is a very transparent and democratic organisation. The Sikh community has organised the Sikh Council, which now has a full-time parliamentary officer in Westminster who helps build awareness and understanding of the Sikh religion. Funded by donations made at Gurdwaras (Sikh places of worship) and subscriptions from other Sikh groups, the Sikh Council provides advice and support to charities and community groups, and, like the Board of Jewish Deputies, has been established on solidly democratic grounds. This is a fantastic example of what we Hindus can – and should – build for ourselves as a community. But our biggest weakness is that British Hindus do not have a united voice. The Hindu Forum has worked hard to fill this gap, but continues to be underfinanced.

Those of us in politics who love this country and who have benefited from its religious and political tolerance should fight for that to continue – this is what has made it such a brilliant place to live. Alas, there have been many examples of those in politics doing exactly the opposite. I was so appalled and outraged by the examples in recent years of antisemitic attitudes in the ranks of senior Labour Party officials and associated activists that I asked for an urgent debate. Having first asked for one in April 2018, I finally managed to secure a debate in September 2018 in the form of a one-hour 'question for short debate' session. The debate was one of the most heavily subscribed in the House of Lords in a very long time. My remarks went viral and I was quickly inundated with messages of support and thanks – not only from Jews in the UK, but also in India, Israel and across the world.

I started my debate by stating that antisemitism concerns us all.

The notion that it is solely a Jewish problem is as dangerous as it is wrong. History is full of powerful words and actions, but silence can be just as formidable. When we are silent in the face of intolerance, we encourage prejudice. When we are silent in the face of false-hoods, we allow lies to become truth. When we are silent in the face of hatred, then we help hate to spread. I recalled the famous words of a German theologian and Lutheran pastor, Martin Niemöller, best known for his opposition to the Nazi regime during the 1930s:

> First they came for the socialists, and I did not speak out – because I was not a socialist. Then they came for the trade unionists, and I did not speak out – because I was not a trade unionist. Then they came for the Jews, and I did not speak out – because I was not a Jew. Then they came for me – and there was no one left to speak for me.

What we must understand here is that hate knows no bounds. We saw that in the horrors of the Holocaust, and we see it now with extremist terrorism and the rise of both the far right and the ultra-left. Antisemitism is a threat that goes beyond Jewish communities and party politics.

For me, this is personal. As a member of the British Hindu community, I understand the pain that prejudice brings. My family and I came to this country from Uganda more than forty-five years ago to escape a brutal dictator, and Britain welcomed us. For us, the Jews were a positive example of what immigrants can achieve by integrating fully into society. In them, we saw people who not only survived horrific persecution but also thrived despite it. Our two communities continue to live side by side, and we have a number of commonalities and shared values. Each attaches importance to hard work, education, enterprise, family and faith. We also share an unshakable loyalty to this great country, the United Kingdom.

If you want an idea of how much Jewish people value their Britishness, I suggest you visit a synagogue, just as the famous diarist Samuel Pepys did in 1663. You will observe, as he did and I myself have done on many occasions, that, during every Sabbath service, the congregation reads out a prayer for the welfare of the royal family and the Prime Minister. What greater expression of patriotism and love of this country? What greater testament to British values of tolerance and compassion from people who have suffered so much throughout history?

Jews have long felt safe in this country. Regardless of what was happening elsewhere in the world, here in the UK – like us Hindus – they felt at home. In the past couple of years, with antisemitism on the rise in France, Hungary and other parts of Europe, many Jews have expressed relief that they are living in Britain and not elsewhere. Even recent growth in recorded antisemitic incidents in this country has not dampened the Jewish community's feeling that they are fundamentally protected by the UK's values, laws and institutions.

However, when my Jewish friends say that they fear for their children's safety in schools, synagogues and universities, when they are afraid of openly identifying as Jewish and when they start to question their future in this country, the rest of us have a duty first to listen and then to ask, 'How has it come to this? Why has it come to this?' And, most importantly, 'What are we going to do about it?'

First, it is essential to uphold the great effort that took place after the Second World War to ensure, through our government and the rule of law, that antisemitism in all its forms will never be tolerated. Secondly, the government must not allow the passage of time to soften our resolve against antisemitism. There is a generation of young people who did not grow up with the same awareness that many of us have of the Holocaust, but they are politicised in other ways. They must understand that hatred of Jews – hatred of any community – is a danger to us all.

I refuse to bear witness to hatred as it eats away at our social and moral fabric. I will stand up for my Jewish friends who love this country, people who have given so much to Britain and who ask for nothing more than to feel protected. All of us – Hindus, Christians, Jews, Muslims, Sikhs and those of no faith – must stand up and speak out for the oppressed, whoever they are and wherever they are. As Pastor Niemöller warned, if we do not look out for each other, no one will look out for us.

When antisemitism does rear its ugly head, it should be condemned across all political parties. What is needed is a willingness to make peace with Israel, not delusional fantasies about a Middle East without Israel. British Asians need to stand up on this issue, as another of our links with Jews is a feeling that 'it could be us next time' – as it was in Uganda.

However, I do not think something like the expulsion from Uganda will ever happen here, despite a small and benighted section of the Labour Party that seems to be doing its best to stoke up antisemitism. The new generation of Asians are fully integrated into, and making an even bigger impact on, British society. They are better educated than people of my father's generation, so things have moved on; they have adopted a British way of doing things and I think they have a great future. They go to university and see each other as British Asians – not necessarily as Punjabi, Gujarati, Bengali and Pakistani. They are united by being British Asians, and have a collectivised sense of political responsibility that coheres around that identity.

Overall, those of immigrant heritage need to acknowledge that (to adapt an old adage) with British freedoms come British responsibilities. When we respect other people's ethnicities and faiths, we in fact show respect to our own; this must happen in a civic context, not a supra-civic context, which is a principle all great religions historically have been able to accommodate, to varying degrees. What is salient about British Hindus, just as it is about Muslims and Sikhs and people of other faiths in Britain, is, as John Major once put it, that 'they respect the law, secular and religious, that they bring children up by earnest moral standards, that they are good citizens'. Ethnic and religious identity should not divide us, but instead bring all of us closer together.

12

SMALL BUSINESS, BIG WORLD

The origins of the current challenging economic climate in Britain can be traced back a long way. For nearly thirty years there has been too much public sector borrowing and too little investment in infrastructure, housing and research; too much reliance on the City of London and service industries; too much regulation, taxation and compliance; the wrong kind of education reform and not enough exporting to high-growth economies. Plus an absolutely terrible planning system, which hamstrings business owners at every turn. We need to stabilise the great economic ship of our country by setting out a credible strategy to bring down the deficit and allow British business to bypass the uncertainties of Brexit.

Small and medium-sized enterprises (SMEs) are one of the keys to righting Britain's economic ship, along with exports. During my time in the House of Lords I helped to establish a select committee, chaired by Lord Cope of Berkeley, that examined ways in which the government could help SMEs to export. Set up in 2012, this committee (in which Lord Haskel was another important member) scored some notable successes, with some of its recommendations being taken on as policy.

SMEs remain a subject close to my heart, given that I have worked to finance so many small businesses and served for two years as a director of Harrow Enterprise Agency. I still think Britain has a long way to go in terms of policy making it easier for small firms to set up and grow, particularly in the area of financing. In some ways, it is more difficult to finance a small firm now than it was in the 1980s, and employment legislation seems to get more complex and onerous with every passing year. We need to make sure we don't regulate Britain's small businesses out of existence.

Britain is one of the only countries in the world where companies have to pay tax to employ people. I understand the logic behind employees paying tax, but an employer having to pay national insurance contributions to employ them is too much.

Immigrants have a big role to play in this, as statistics show that they are far more likely to be entrepreneurial than their British-born counterparts. The 2015 Global Entrepreneurship Monitor (GEM), which analysed early-stage start-up activity across the UK, found that immigrants are the people most likely to start businesses in Britain. A separate study, conducted in 2013 by the Centre for Entrepreneurs and company data business Duedil, found that migrant entrepreneurs are behind one in seven UK companies. The report also revealed that they start their businesses much younger than their indigenous counterparts – at an average age of forty-four compared with fifty-two.

Whatever their original culture, British entrepreneurs face significant challenges that we need to address as a society. Financing of SMEs remains a really big issue, despite the £20 billion National Loan Guarantee Scheme set up by the Cameron government in 2012. Whenever I speak to small business owners, I still hear about the difficulties they are having with financing, so much that it almost makes me think I need to get back into something like Fast Finance!

Having run a business and corporate finance practice for many years, I know how difficult it can be to get finance in tough times, and how finance is needed not only to help firms survive, but also to grow and invest. We have established the Enterprise Finance Guarantee Scheme to help viable businesses that have insufficient collateral, and we also have the Start-Up Loans Scheme, which provides advice and start-up finance for young entrepreneurs looking to establish and then grow a business.

Nonetheless, a better solution is needed. I believe governments should look into encouraging the creation of new banks – particularly local and regional banks – something that helped to drive economic growth when I first got into business. In addition, I believe the government should consider granting full banking licences to other international banks who are cash rich, such as those from India and China who do not currently do large amounts of business in the UK. Increased competition on lending will undoubtedly help to drive economic growth. We also need to encourage and support the growth of financial methods that don't rely on the banks (including peer-to-peer lending schemes) to boost the amount of finance available.

In the 1970s, there were a large number of finance companies – licensed under the Consumer Credit Act – that provided business finance to small and micro businesses. Companies such as Forward Trust specialised in specific industries, and because of their expertise were able to take risks that banks wouldn't. I hope future governments will look at how we can resurrect such invaluable services to help meet the lending needs of SMEs in the modern economy.

I must pay tribute to our excellent former Chancellor George Osborne, who understood that what we need is more competition in the banking sector and we must therefore water down requirements for banking licences. I welcome the newly formed challenger banks, which have a large number of British Indian and SME customers.

Then there is the issue of compliance. Since 1998, the total cost of regulation imposed on business each year has been almost £90 billion – a staggeringly high figure. Like many businessmen, I have been encouraged to hear the plans of successive governments to reduce this figure, but it never seems to happen in reality. Tough decisions have unfortunately been delayed and the strategic approach to the economy is left wanting.

There is a hope that real freedom of enterprise may come with Brexit but the problem is deeper than adherence to European legislation; we should not fool ourselves on that. The regulatory burden on small business is as much a home-grown problem as a European one.

In 2011, George Osborne described our planning system as 'a chronic obstacle to economic growth'. He's still right. We must ensure that our small businesses do not continue to invest thousands in consultants, lawyers and architects, only to fall at the final hurdle because of anti-growth attitudes in town halls across the country. And this doesn't apply to only small businesses. I remember Lord Wolfson, chief executive of Next, once stating that he could not spend the £100 million he had set aside for investment because he couldn't get planning permission. While Next is obviously not a small retailer, this is a clear example of an ambitious firm's economic activity being held back by a planning system not fit for purpose.

Exports are the other part of the picture. Perhaps the greatest economic problem we have in Britain is our balance of trade deficit. The country simply does not have enough exports to pay for its imports. But the problem isn't that we are lacking the right things to export; every year I sit on a judging panel for the Queen's Awards for Exports and, reviewing the applications, I see amazing products and clever marketing and export strategies that generate huge amounts of business. Instead, the problem seems to be that, in terms of export markets, most of these companies are too regional. The number of British firms that only focus on the European Union is staggering, which is odd considering that Europe is the one continent in the world with sluggish growth and an ageing population. You get the odd firm exporting to North America, a few to China and some focusing on Saudi Arabia, but I don't recall seeing a single application to the Queen's Awards talking about Africa, nor very many targeting the emerging economies of Asia and South America.

This is why, for all the difficulties it presents, Brexit also offers an opportunity – to challenge assumptions and change our world view in order that a more energetic conception of export markets becomes second nature to British businesses.

Again, this is an area where immigrants can both help and benefit: they can exploit their links with the wider world in a more open, ambitious export market. The state also has a role in strengthening those links, in my view. As Chancellor, George Osborne widened UK Export Finance's remit (UK Export Finance is the ministerial body that supports British exporters, providing credit and advice) so it could support all types of exports, and I asked the relevant department to launch new short-term export-finance products, aimed particularly at supporting smaller firms. These materialised in the form of a Bond Support Scheme, an Export Working Capital Scheme and a Foreign Exchange Credit Support Scheme.

Indeed, in recent years there have been notable examples of UK Export Finance helping British companies win, finance and fulfil contracts, but the UK's share of the world's global export market is still too low. While big firms find it relatively easy to access foreign markets, SMEs have real problems in doing so. If they export at all, they tend to export to familiar markets, such as the eurozone, rather than high-growth markets such as China and India (with Africa soon to join them). We need a culture change.

UK trade missions to other countries often produce excellent results, but I think it is vital that we review the diplomatic support our companies receive overseas. The British government has in the past indicated a preference for more businesspeople to be involved in diplomacy, and I think this would be a welcome move to help prioritise growth. Our international competitors are regularly knocking at the door of other countries. We cannot afford to be left behind because there is a lack of business knowledge at the heart of government.

We also need to consider the transport and infrastructure needed to help SMEs export; our competitors are increasing their airport capacities as new markets open, and so should we. The introduction of a national roads strategy is a welcome addition, as is the 2012 Pension Infrastructure Platform, which has brought an initial £2 billion investment in UK infrastructure.

The most important thing is to make sure that our actions match our rhetoric, and that we demonstrate that not only is Britain open for business, but that we are a nation which thrives on seeking out new economic opportunities. It is often disheartening to read press

The Popat family ahead of a function in 2014; the name 'Popat' literally translates to 'parrot'.

Mark Fletcher's art deco-inspired wedding in March 2016. (*Left to right*: Ameet, Mark, his husband, Will, Sandhya and Dolar.)

The Popat brothers and their wives at a family wedding. (*Left to right*: Kantesh, Rekha, Pankaj, Nisha, Dolar, Sandhya, Manoj and Illa Popat.)

Dolar and Sandhya meeting the Queen at London's Guildhall, 2016.

Dolar representing the UK on trade envoy duties at the Global African Investment Summit in Kigali, September 2016, with President Museveni of Uganda (*left*) and President Kagame of Rwanda (*middle*).

Dolar playing golf with his friend Giles Foden, author of *The Last King of Scotland*, against the backdrop of Tororo Rock, his first time back to the golf course since childhood.

BELOW Back to school: Dolar sits in his former classroom at Rock View School in Tororo, Uganda.

Sandhya with Dolar outside his childhood home in Busolwe, during a visit in 2017.

ABOVE Ameet Jogia, Dolar and Sandhya's 'fourth son', at his wedding to Priya Jatania at the House of Lords. (*Back row, left to right*: Sandhya, Rupeen, Dolar, Shivaan and Rupa Popat.)

LEFT Rupeen and Rupa's civil wedding at the Houses of Parliament. (*Left to right*: Paavan, Sandhya, Rupeen, Rupa, Dolar and Shivaan.)

coverage of businesses in Britain, which treat profit as something to be avoided. The media also needs to get on board, changing people's mindsets, so that we can really give businesses, entrepreneurs and investors the confidence to grow our economy.

One should not be too gloomy, of course. In 1953, the value of the UK's exported goods and services was £3.7 billion; in 2019 that figure is over £600 billion. This is a sign of how much the UK has opened up in terms of international trade – even when one factors in inflation and all the other relevant factors that diminish the bare discrepancy between those two numbers.

Currently, a recent slight increase in exports of goods to non-EU countries is encouraging for a post-Brexit world. The UK Trade and Investment (now the Department for International Trade) was given a boost of £140 million under the Cameron government, including £26 million specifically for exporting SMEs. The funds go through the department to help companies make contacts and sell to overseas markets. There is more money available for SMEs to attend trade shows abroad through expanding the Tradeshow Access Programme. Substantial discounts are also being offered on the Overseas Market Introduction Service, which provides targeted market research to help businesses find those crucial first contacts overseas and to help them develop relationships in new, fast-growing markets.

All this is encouraging, but it is now important that we maintain the momentum through the Brexit process, delivering tangible business opportunities that benefit SMEs across all sectors and all regions.

I just mentioned Britain's export value in the early 1950s. There are things that we can learn from that decade that many have forgotten. In the late '50s and early '60s there was a tremendous spirit of dawning optimism and a focus on the future. Things had been difficult, to say the least. Austerity is a much-used word now; it was very much a reality then. The difficulties, though, were seen as a challenge to overcome. All of us, in government and in business, need to be aware of the difficult times we live in and the choices we face.

There are, as I see it, two dangers to growth: pessimism and apathy. Accepting that UK exports are fairly strong, but could be better, risks leaving us in the doldrums. To concentrate excessively on the difficulties of achieving or sustaining growth risks leading to anaemic growth. We all need to be bolder, both in making policy and in making business decisions. Government can be risk-averse, but so too can business and investors. Confidence and optimism have led to growth and prosperity in the past and they are what we need now. Indeed, there would be a further dividend in making Britain a confident, prosperous exporting country: the encouragement of inward investment.

This process of boosting exports, by SMEs in particular, and encouraging overseas investors to come to the UK requires close cooperation between the Department for Business, Energy and Industrial Strategy and the Foreign and Commonwealth Office. Personally, and not surprisingly given my background, I have always thought we need to focus harder on the Commonwealth, in particular Africa.

This is partly the role of the new Department for International Trade, which more generally is responsible for striking and extending trade agreements between the United Kingdom and non-EU states. I applaud Theresa May for creating this new body in Whitehall shortly after she took office in 2016 following the United Kingdom's vote to leave the European Union.

For those of us who have argued for many years that we have

neglected the Commonwealth, leaving the European Union offers us an historic opportunity to reshape our foreign policy and rekindle relations with this amazing group of nations. I am very fond of quoting Lord Howell, who often sits just near me in the House of Lords: 'Europe is our region, America our ally and the Commonwealth our family.'

I agree that the Commonwealth should be seen as Britain's family, and as with members of all families, those in the Commonwealth are all different yet united by strong foundations – none stronger than the incredible leadership of the Queen. However, these foundations risk crumbling unless there is constant renovation, and sometimes we have failed in that, despite Her Majesty's best efforts.

I want to ponder for a few moments on where we have gone wrong. I think that there are four main problems. First, successive UK governments gave little thought to how we could make the Commonwealth an effective trading body. Many of our ministers and civil servants feared Britain playing a leading role in the organisation because of the risk of creating a 'colonial' dynamic. This is both nonsense and cowardice.

Secondly, the signing of a new Commonwealth charter in 2012 was meant to give this 'family of nations' a new direction. The members agreed to prioritise democracy and human rights. However, this has not worked, because in doing so we prioritised something contentious over trade, where there is very little dispute. That is not to say we should not trumpet and try to actualise the civic values that are at the core of the Commonwealth. We should. But in a climate of competing national and commercial interests, trade is the best way to begin the conversation on rights and values, not the other way round.

Thirdly, our membership of the European Union consumed a vast and disproportionate amount of diplomatic time and resources without delivering an equivalent amount of benefits.

Finally, our membership of the European single market and customs union has engendered apathy in many of our businesses. British businesses that have created what should be world-leading products have limited themselves to exporting to only our nearest trading partners and neglected emerging markets and the Commonwealth – the places we really need to be focusing on.

If we are to give the Commonwealth purpose, let us focus first on trade. The Commonwealth comprises fifty-three largely English-speaking countries, with a combined population of 2.6 billion. It covers a third of the globe, has a combined GDP of more than $10 trillion and includes five G20 countries, with trade projected to surpass $1 trillion by 2020. Given that Britain's trade deficit of £40 billion is the greatest economic challenge our country currently faces, we should bear in mind that a recent report highlighted that it is 19 per cent cheaper on average for a business in the Commonwealth to trade because of commonalities such as our legal system and language. By reforming the Commonwealth around a trade agenda, we would both solve one of our biggest problems and help to spread prosperity. Trade is of mutual benefit – for not just one but both countries concerned.

While there are many things we can do at Commonwealth level to build trade links between members, there is also bilateral work we should be doing. At the moment, not all Commonwealth countries have trade envoys, such as my role as the Prime Minister's trade envoy to Uganda and Rwanda, or that of Pauline Latham MP, for Kenya. We should appoint trade envoys to *all* Commonwealth countries as a matter of urgency.

The trade envoy programme not only offers Britain a unique opportunity to build bridges with Commonwealth nations but also allows government representatives to spend time on issues with their foreign counterparts that ministers simply cannot always get to. As I write, we are planning to double trade with Uganda and increase it in Rwanda by even more. This won't be easy, but it's what we should be aiming for.

There are also other steps we can take. Our aviation links with African Commonwealth countries are woeful. In 2015, having operated these routes for over sixty years, British Airways made the shameful decision to suspend flights to and from Dar es Salaam, Entebbe and Lusaka, among others. Those flights were almost always full and were our bridge to these nations, so I hope other providers will step in and replace them. However, a replacement is difficult because there are currently no slots available at either Gatwick or Heathrow. We often talk about aviation policy in the House of Lords, but in a post-Brexit world we will definitely need to be focusing more on increased connectivity. We are probably around thirty years behind where we should be. When I see what other countries are doing in aviation, I am ashamed of our faint-heartedness.

Similarly, the decision in 2017 taken by Barclays to sell its African trading arm should be seen as a national scandal. Barclays had been in Africa for over 100 years and its brand is beyond compare; and yet, because of legislation passed – to my eternal regret – in the House of Lords, it is selling away one of our great connections. That harms the great brand of UK PLC.

I end this chapter with the idea of a Commonwealth bank or, more fittingly, the 'Queen Elizabeth Commonwealth Bank'. Collective institutions bind organisations together. We already have a

World Bank and a European Central Bank, so why not a Commonwealth Bank? I have in mind something like the Asian Infrastructure Investment Bank (of which Britain is a founding member), an organisation that could transform economic development across the Commonwealth, supporting major infrastructure projects and possibly also lending directly to businesses.

As I see on my many travels in Africa and elsewhere, across the Commonwealth there is now a huge appetite for new infrastructure investment. New roads, rail and energy projects are all essential to economic development. A Commonwealth bank would be a great way of demonstrating our commitment to our family, showing that Britain is still an outward-looking nation. Such a bank would help all its members, particularly the poorest.

Let us be bold in our approach to the Commonwealth; let us unite around increasing trade, investment and cultural links and let Britain lead the charge for a Commonwealth bank. It would not only bring the Commonwealth together in a shared purpose, but would also be the most fitting tribute to Her Majesty's magnificent leadership of this wonderful family of nations.

13

DESTINATION INTEGRATION: INDIA, MODI AND MORE

As a result of my political, business, religious and family interests, I continue to travel widely. An important reason for travelling has been my work – first as a Conservative Party activist and later a minister – trying to build trade links between Britain and India, both on the basis of shared colonial history and significant immigration of Indians to Britain.

At the same time as fostering an international connection with India, I have always tried to keep in touch with key leaders in the wider Indian community in Britain, for instance acting as strategic advisor to the Hindu Forum, or setting up the Conservative Friends of India. It's important that we all keep trumpeting the positive impact that Indians – not just Hindus, of course, but Muslims, Sikhs, Jains, Zoroastrians, Christians and people from other faiths – have had on this country.

Others might disagree, but it seems to me that it's tremendously important to stay on the highway to integration at both an international and a national level. The forces against integration are sometimes challenging but the rewards are clear to see, whether one is talking about the benefits British Indians have brought to our country, the impact of investment from India in Britain or the role that Britain can play in fostering good relations, in both politics and trade, between itself, India and other countries.

The British Indian community is one of the largest ethnic minority communities in the UK, with the 2011 census recording 1.5 million people of Indian origin living in the country, which equates to approximately 2.4 per cent of the British population – the third largest group after 'white British' and 'any other white'. (This is a two-way relationship – there are some 51,000 British nationals currently living in India.)

British Indians make up the largest sub-group of British Asians and are one of the largest Indian communities in the Indian diaspora. The British Indian community is divided approximately as follows: 950,000 Gujaratis; 550,000 Sikhs/Punjabis; 60,000 Jains; 10,000 Buddhists; and 30,000 from other groups, including Tamils, Goans and Parsis.

The origins of today's Indian diaspora in Britain date back to the period of British rule in India (1858–1947). It was predominately the Parsi community of Gujarat and Bengal who were the first settlers in Britain, arriving here in the eighteenth and nineteenth centuries as qualified doctors and lawyers. The Parsi community enjoyed significant prominence in Britain in those early days; Dadabhai Naoroji, a successful Parsi businessman, was elected as the first Britain Indian Member of Parliament as far back as 1892.

The largest wave of Indian settlers came to the UK after Indian independence in 1947. Workers, predominantly from the Punjab region, filled vacancies in the British industrial and manufacturing sector. The second wave of migrants, as I have mentioned, was mainly made up of Gujaratis who came from east Africa in the 1960s and 1970s, often fleeing very difficult circumstances.

Second- and third-generation British Indians no longer feel like immigrants in this country, and have firmly made their mark on Britain. They include politicians Priti Patel, Shailesh Vara, Alok Sharma, Rishi Sunak, Suella Fernandes and Ranil Jayawardena; members of the extremely influential Hinduja family; and the prominent industrialist Lakshmi Mittal.

Both the Hinduja family and Lakshmi Mittal regularly head the *Sunday Times* Rich List, but they are far from the only British Indians to appear, with Anil Agarwal, Bikhu and Vijay Patel, Mike Jatania and many more also featuring. In banking, too, there are serious British Indian players, among them Tushar Morzaria (group finance director, Barclays) and Baroness Vadera (chief executive of Santander). And in media businesses, figures such as Arti Lukha, Sima Kotecha, Sejal Karia, Seema Jaspal and Manali Lukha are making their presence felt.

With my background, I'm obviously interested in those making waves in politics, including figures such as Meenal Sachdev, Reena Ranger OBE, Resham Kotecha, Hiten Ganatra, Abhishek Sachdev – as well as my own aide, Ameet Jogia.

British Indians have also excelled at sport, Monty Panesar and Ravi Bopara being just two examples. In entertainment, young British Indian pop star Jay Sean has topped both the UK and US charts with several hits. Notable British Indian actors include Ben Kingsley, Meera Syall, Sanjeev Bhaskar, Jimi Mistry and Dev Patel, the star of the film *Slumdog Millionaire*. British Indian producer and director Gurinder Chadha (famous for *Bend It Like Beckham*) is another figure at the top level of the British film industry.

Over 70 per cent of British Indians own their own home, giving the community the highest homeownership rate by ethnicity in Britain. In addition, 65 per cent of British Indians attend a top university. British Indians are also more likely to be married than those from the country's other ethnic groups, as well as more likely to be self-employed and (thank goodness!) less likely to go to prison.

Shortly after the second wave of migration in the '60s and '70s, the Indian community's natural expertise in trade and business began to make them shopkeepers in the 'nation of shopkeepers' almost overnight, and curry has gradually replaced fish and chips as Britain's favourite dish. Such examples reflect the benefits and results of sharing experiences and bringing communities together.

Today's Indian diaspora in the UK is dominated by a completely new, hybrid generation. Born in Britain but still rooted by their rich, Indian heritage, these British-born Indians are the product of the hard work of their parents and grandparents. It is now firmly established in Britain, excelling in almost every profession from banking, business, sports, media and politics to medicine and life sciences.

By any metric, British Indians have changed Britain for the better. In economic terms alone this community outperforms all others, with that 2.4 per cent of the population producing over 6 per cent of British GDP. Culturally, economically and socially, I think Britain is a better place because of us. In almost every industry, you see British Indians at the top. One in eight workers in the City of London is of Indian origin; eighty of the richest 1,000 people in Britain are Indian; we have one of the lowest divorce rates in Britain; we care for and respect our elderly; and our communities build and run temples and community centres to bring people together. Alongside the thousands of small businesses in this country run by Indians, we now have so many of our children succeeding in myriad other professions.

For a diaspora of 1.5 million, all of this is very impressive – but it is not all about business and money. We saw something of this when prominent members of the Hindu and Sikh communities joined David Cameron at a special reception at Downing Street to celebrate Diwali in 2011. Sandhya helped with the preparations and managed the decoration of No. 10 splendidly.

Speaking at the event, David Cameron paid tribute to the great contribution Indians have made to the UK, and to illustrate, noted the ArcelorMittal Orbit, the Olympic Park sculpture designed by Anish Kapoor. Lakshmi Mittal funded it, but the important thing (and I am sure Lakshmi would agree with me) was that this was art of the highest quality, created by a British Indian. Cameron also noted that Indians were serving in the British Army and he had recently met one on a visit to the frontline at Garmsir in Afghanistan. In fact, British Indians are the second highest represented ethnic minority in the British Army. Indian achievement in this country clearly extends well beyond the business world.

Overall, then, the Indian's immigrant experience in Britain has been an amazing success story. I think that in large part this is because British and Indians values are generally so similar, in their focus on family, community, faith, education and commerce. It's a very good marriage!

The British Indian community's achievements are a direct result of its members treating Britain as their home, and being proud to be British. There has been a focus on genuine integration. But we have been happy to make this country our home because Britain has given us so many opportunities to do well.

This model of successful integration has also had political implications. The Conservative Party, in particular, has recognised that the British Indian community is an essential part of modern Britain, which ultimately led to the formation of the Conservative Friends of India.

But the Indian population in the UK is unique in the sense that its relationship between the two countries works both ways – it is not simply about British Indians living in the UK but also about Britain's role in India. The diaspora has evolved into a special relationship that is expressed in a number of different areas, including trade and investment. This extends from corner-shop owners importing and exporting goods to ventures involving some of the largest companies in the world.

Today, the single largest manufacturing employer in the UK is the Indian conglomerate Tata, which owns Jaguar Land Rover and Corus Steel, and employs approximately 47,000 people. There are many other British Indian success stories, including FTSE 100 companies such as Vedanta and the Hinduja Group.

Meanwhile, the British company Vodafone is the third-largest telecom service provider in India and has the fastest growing subscriber base there. Vodafone has 100 million customers in India – almost five times its UK customer base. Further, the 2011 deal between BP and the Indian company Reliance was worth £7.2 billion and is currently one of the largest direct investments by a foreign company in India.

A recent report released by Anuj Chande of Grant Thornton detailed the phenomenal successes Indian investors are now achieving in Britain. The report states how a record 842 Indian companies are now operating in the UK, which employ over 100,000 people and have combined revenues of £48 billion. Indian investors are increasingly seeing Britain's business-friendly environment, world-class universities and cultural highlights as the best place to create an overseas base.

This is incredibly encouraging for those of us who have long wanted Britain and India to develop closer economic and political ties. Building better relations with India was David Cameron's first foreign policy priority when he took over as Prime Minister and we are now beginning to feel the benefits of his and Osborne's foresight.

But it also takes two hands to clap, and Narendra Modi's government have been alive to the economic benefits of building relations with Britain, particularly in a post-Brexit environment. Modi took the unusual step for an Indian Prime Minister of attending last year's Commonwealth Heads of Government Meeting in London, as well as his official visit in November 2015.

During those visits he was able to negotiate several key policies to assist Indian interests in Britain, including a fast-track system to resolve issues that Indian companies face in the UK and a new UK–India Tech Alliance to develop new technologies. These are in addition to the existing research relationship between both na-tions and the high-priority India–UK trade partnership discussions to create an even more positive post-Brexit relationship. India's outstanding economic growth in recent years has been in marked contrast to a lot of the world's economic struggles, particularly in Europe. The headwinds against economic success have been strong: a potential US–China trade war, the financial crisis and the eurozone debt issues – not to mention Brexit uncertainties – have led to many leading economies slowing and protectionism rearing its ugly head again.

Britain's economy has also done remarkably well to weather the storm. Unemployment – currently at 3.8 per cent – is down to the lowest level the UK has seen since the 1970s, with a record high of 32.7 million people in work. The British economy has now grown by over 17 per cent since 2010, outperforming most other advanced economies. Investment in the UK is also booming, with recent OECD figures revealing that Britain was the most popular country in Europe for foreign direct investment (FDI).

India has played a big part in that success, with Department for International Trade figures showing that 120 new FDI projects in 2017–18 originated in India, creating nearly 6,000 new jobs. Leading Indian investors like Tata Steel are now being joined by newer firms like TMF Metal Holdings, Route Mobile and BB Ltd, who in turn are finding unprecedented levels of success.

These investors are attracted to Britain because of lower tax thresholds, a business-friendly environment, good access to finance and the fall in the value of sterling following the Brexit referendum result. But, in turn, these companies are helping to create jobs, build links between our two great nations, give our workforce more skills and hugely contributing through taxes, with a record £684 million paid in corporation tax by Indian businesses in the UK last year.

Whether it be in pharmaceuticals, IT, engineering and manufacturing, or business and financial services, these investments are both helping the British economy to move on from the financial crisis and showing the way towards a post-Brexit future. Government borrowing is now down to its lowest level in seventeen years, and Britain is moving away from this period of austerity and back into a mind-set where it can invest properly in the future.

As it stands, trade between Britain and India in goods and

services is a little over £15 billion. This figure has the potential to increase significantly in years ahead, particularly if Indian investors and high-net-worth individuals continue to see Britain – and in particular London – as the best place for a second home.

Long-term trade and diplomatic links between Britain and India are, of course, intricately tied up with the colonial past. I think that the history of the British Empire is always going to provoke mixed opinions, but ultimately I think it was a positive for the world. Nobody can argue that it was all pleasant and beneficial – quite the opposite in the experience of millions of colonised people – but the Empire brought many benefits nonetheless. These benefits should not be swept under the carpet, just as historical abuses should not be covered up. In the case of India and Britain, our history binds us together through a shared language, a shared democracy and parliamentary system, and a shared rule of law, among other things.

Britain wants to see India develop and grow, and hopefully we can work together for many years to show that democracy – as well as the pursuit of both prosperity and happiness – is the way forward.

Trade is the key to this joint future. I always knew I could help David Cameron with this and, as our relationship grew, he was happy to accept my advice. I accompanied him on his first major trip to India as Prime Minister in February 2013.

I think the symbolic intent of that trip was to rekindle the British relationship with India, but to do things in a different way. We have ministers visiting India almost every month on all matters, but trade remains our first priority. I think we've seen a lot of progress, but there is still a lot more we can do. There is huge untapped business potential in India, with 1.2 billion customers for British goods.

We simply have so much that we can gain from one another. India is set to be the world's third largest economy by 2030, but needs assistance in sectors like construction, infrastructure and finance. As I outlined in the previous chapter, Britain needs to rebalance its economy away from household consumption and the City and towards exports – and it has particular expertise in many of the sectors that India is lacking in. Working together will undoubtedly boost both countries.

Cameron also went to India in November 2013, and then again in November 2015. I joined him in February 2013, and I think I'm right in saying we were part of the largest trade delegation Britain had ever sent to another country. India's focus on higher education, finance and infrastructure tallies with Britain's expertise in those fields, so we were able to bring the right people with the right experience and contacts and put them in a room with their Indian counterparts. But it is never just about the trip itself; there are always a lot of follow-up meetings and deals done afterwards. The trip itself is really just a catalyst for further discussion.

During the 2015 delegation, businessmen and politicians from both sides discussed the opportunities available for further collaboration. Research is one area where we are India's ideal partners. Since the delegation, the UK and India have jointly committed over £100 million for research projects in the areas of health, energy, climate change and water.

These prime ministerial visits were part of a long-term Conservative Party plan to engage with India. It is also worth pointing out the long relationship the Labour Party has had with the Congress Party, which dominated relations between the UK and India for many years, so it was a changing of the guards at both ends.

The backdrop to these visits in opposition was the breaking off of relations between Britain and Narendra Modi in 2002, after internecine violence between Hindus and Muslims in Gujarat when Modi was the state's Chief Minister. While the government of Gujarat is generally considered to have been – to an extent – complicit in the riots, Modi's own role is a matter of much debate. He saw it, rightly in my view, as a situation characterised by an uncontrollable chain of action and reaction. The European Union and many Western nations reacted negatively to the violence, without a clear understanding of the complex issues at play on the ground. India's Supreme Court later cleared Modi of complicity in the killings – albeit with a ruling challenged by some Indian Muslims.

Some on the left know this. As Lord Parekh (a leading voice on human rights and an eminent political philosopher) put it, as the lifting of the ban on relations between Britain and Gujarat was being discussed:

> An equally sensible attitude is increasingly being taken with reference to Gujarat, the Indian state from which I come, where genocide took place in February 2002, when a large number of Muslims were killed with the complicity of the state. The American government denied a visa to the Chief Minister but the British government took a very sensible view and said nothing. Increasingly, the British government began to recognise that we had no conclusive evidence that the Chief Minister had been directly and actively involved in what had gone on; after all, he had been in power for only four months. Nor did we ignore the fact that this sort of thing had happened in other parts of India, and therefore we could not single out one state alone.[6]

---

6   Hansard, HL Deb, 21 November 2013, vol. 749, col. 1077.

The decision to break off links after 2002 was taken by a Labour government; it was the Conservative Party that pushed very strongly to change the situation when it returned to power. Gujarat has been peaceful since 2002, although what happened was obviously very sad indeed and it will take time for the scars to heal. There are 950,000 Gujaratis living in the UK (the second largest number of Gujaratis living outside of India) and Britain does a lot of trade with Gujarat, so it made sense to be back in harness. I and a number of my colleagues in the Conservative Party pushed very strongly for re-engagement, and I was delighted when it happened.

Re-engagement was the consequence of months and months of campaigning through the Foreign Office, featuring letters, appeals and meetings with the then Foreign Office minister Lord Howell. I also reiterated the importance of reconnecting with Modi to David Cameron when we were travelling to India together.

I still remember the day I received a call from No. 10 to say that Britain would be re-engaging with Modi. I was driving back from the Conservative Party conference in Birmingham with Jitesh (now Lord) Gadhia and Ameet Jogia. The call was the start of a fruitful and strong new relationship between Britain and Modi.

It is also worth mentioning Modi's record in Gujarat – one of the few states with reliable electricity and lower levels of corruption – of lots of investment, high employment and the creation of a generally very pro-business environment.

Modi became Prime Minister in 2014 after getting Indian people out to vote in record numbers. He was the first Indian Prime Minister to have a Twitter account and now has nearly 16 million followers, making him the third most-followed politician after former US President Barack Obama and current US President

Donald Trump. The global reach of Modi's social media is partly why many in the Indian diaspora feel closer to him than previous Indian leaders.

However, a lot of the British media coverage of Modi's victory was negative. My Conservative parliamentary colleague, Priti Patel MP, wrote to a number of newspapers about it and she was right: the British press had unfairly tainted Modi. I have to say that the British Indian population saw it differently to the media; there were victory parties everywhere when the results were announced. We just knew that Modi's election was good for India and for its relations with Britain.

David Cameron was, I think, the first Western leader to phone and congratulate Modi, and there remains a real excitement about what India's future holds. Modi's priority is to get India's economy running back to its full potential, and Britain can play a part in that. Because of the City, we have tremendous expertise that can help finance some of the work that needs to happen. There is an export factor here, too. We have universities hoping to open campuses in India, as well as healthcare providers and insurance companies all wanting to make inroads into India. Many initiatives have been put off either through legislation or fear of corruption, but I think the Modi government has shown itself better at dealing with those issues than many of its predecessors.

From the outset of his premiership, David Cameron really understood the importance of India. He was explicit about this at the G20 summit in Australia in 2014 when he said that building relations with India had become Britain's number-one priority in terms of foreign policy. When Modi came to power, he was determined to secure an official visit.

Luckily, I was in a position to help with this. I had met Modi twice, once in Ahmedabad in 2014 with the British High Commissioner and another time in Delhi. He seemed to me a very humble and dedicated man.

By now, even die-hard anti-Modi figures such as Jeremy Corbyn had performed U-turns and dropped their opposition to his visiting the UK, indeed going so far as to join him for a private meeting. I think this is the first time Corbyn has come round to my way of thinking!

After lunch with the Queen at Buckingham Palace and official talks with David Cameron, Modi addressed a rally at Wembley Stadium to mark the Indian diaspora's contribution to the UK. The rally was spearheaded by one of Modi's close supporters, Manoj Ladwa. Speaking on stage, mainly in Hindi, to a 60,000-strong crowd, Modi hailed India's 'special relationship' with the UK.

It was a real celebration of British Indian culture. The key theme of Modi's speech was aspiration, both for resident and non-resident Indians. To huge cheers, Modi said, 'I would like to assure you that the dreams you have dreamt – and the dreams every Indian has dreamt – India is capable of fulfilling these dreams. There is no reason for India to remain a poor country.' He also spoke of the contribution Indians have made to Britain, perhaps thinking of the inclusiveness agenda he is now trying to effect in India itself.

Modi is extending this agenda internationally, with remarkable effect. His visit to Israel in July 2017 was an historic moment for relations between India and Israel, and marked the end of a long period without public engagement between the two countries (though there had been much going on beneath the surface for some years).

Greeting Modi with obvious warmth at Ben Gurion Airport, Prime Minister Netanyahu told him, 'We have waited seventy years for you.'

There was clearly chemistry between the two leaders, and business was done swiftly as a result. The visit saw Indian and Israeli companies sign strategic pacts worth $4.3 billion, as well as the two countries agreeing a joint science research fund of $40 million, a range of measures transferring Israeli defense technologies and joint security measures against terrorism.

As my friend C. B. Patel put it:

There has been a shift in one of the major tectonic plates of geopolitics. For decades past Indian governments have been out of sync with the Indian public, which held Israel in high esteem, whose remarkable achievements commanded unstinted respect and admiration. The Indo-Israel relationship is no longer to be hidden in a closet; it is out in the open ... The region and the countries farther afield will have to factor the India–Israel strategic partnership into their policies.[7]

This is true, and not only in a negative way, because India has warm relationships with all the major players in the Middle East – Iran, the UAE, Kuwait, Qatar, Saudi Arabia and Egypt – some of whom are either at odds with each other or with Israel. In fact, Modi had visited many of these countries in the run-up to his trip to Israel. The prospect of India brokering peace and trade agreements where others have failed now becomes a real and welcome possibility.

---

7   C. B. Patel, 'Modi's game changing Israeli odyssey', *Asian Voice*, 15 July 2017, p.3.

To celebrate Modi's visit, I and the honorary president of the Conservative Friends of Israel, Lord Polak, hosted a lunch in the House of Lords with the Indian High Commissioner (His Excellency Y. K. Sinha) and the Israeli Ambassador (His Excellency Mark Regev) to the United Kingdom.

We came together to celebrate links between our three countries, which are all committed to similar values. Although Britain was not on Modi's official visit itinerary, we stand on the international stage alongside both Israel and India as their allies and partners. Britain is very fortunate to have strong relations with both of those great countries, and their success is our success.

Another reason to celebrate this shift in world politics is one I have already emphasised several times, which is that the British Indian community and the British Jewish community have a tremendous amount in common. We British Indians have so often looked to the Jewish community for inspiration; the way they have settled, integrated and become successful as immigrants in this country has provided a model that we have emulated.

At a time when so much focus is put on immigration, integration and identity, it is worth pausing and considering the tremendous strides the national communities in Britain, India and Israel have taken towards inclusion – against much greater odds in India and Israel than in Britain, I would say. As with the question of democracy in Africa, one has to look clearly at the conditions in which good intentions are being exercised.

That said, the journey to inclusiveness here for British Indians hasn't always been an easy one. It isn't so long ago that political discussions about identity revolved around, of all things, cricket. Former chairman of the Conservative Party Norman (now Lord)

Tebbit coined the 'cricket test' or 'Tebbit test' in April 1990 in an interview with the *LA Times*. He referred to the 'lack of loyalty' of many immigrants from parts of Asia and the Caribbean to the England cricket team, and said that a large proportion of Britain's Asian population failed to pass the test: which side do they cheer for? Are you still harking back to where you came from or support-ing where you are? I do think British Indians and Pakistanis should always cheer for England, but not everyone agrees with me. And I guess if people feel the urge to celebrate a superb catch from either side in a cricket match, is that so bad? Nevertheless, it is safe to say that Britain's ethnic minorities have definitely become more fully integrated since the 1990s.

People change their minds, anyhow, just like Jeremy Corbyn did on Modi. We need to allow for that whether the person is a political opponent or a political ally. Indeed, flexibility and an openness to change what had previously been a fixed position is one of the most important drivers of successful integration, for both the immigrant and the indigenous host. Lord Tebbit himself wrote to me ahead of a debate about Uganda that I hosted in the Lords in December 2012 to commemorate the fortieth anniversary of the expulsion of Ugandan Asians. He had originally opposed their coming to Britain, but said in his letter, 'It is clear that the Ugandan Asian community has become integrated into Britain and upholds British values and standards.'

The community has, Tebbit went on, 'made a remarkable con-tribution to our economy and the Chancellor's tax revenues and a below average call on his expenditure.'

Britain and India share a rich history and I hope and believe we will all share a prosperous future. As we reflect on how far our nations have progressed since independence and the partition of India in 1947, Britons should be proud to say that we are making good progress in becoming India's partners of choice, as opposed to India's partners of convenience. The same goes for Pakistan. Long may this special relationship continue, and long may British citizens with roots in the Indian subcontinent feel included in British society.

With luck and time, we may even arrive at a situation in which Britain is involved in a new accord between India and Pakistan. It's always very interesting for an oldster like me to listen in when accomplished young professionals with Asian heritage in all three nations meet at a party or a business function. I am constantly struck by how much they want to move on from the divisions of the past into a joint future based on mutual growth and shared values. This sort of attitude makes me very hopeful.

Trade is one important way to help India and Pakistan move on. During a visit to Islamabad in 2011 with a delegation from the Commonwealth Parliamentary Association, I spoke on how countries can trade their way out of poverty and division, and how trade can heal differences. I am pleased to say that in recent years the value of trade between Pakistan and India has increased from $1 billion to over $4 billion. I stressed in my speech that Pakistan's focus should be on trade, and that both nations should move beyond the long and painful era marked by tensions in Kashmir.

Many of these kinds of tensions come down to the question of joining or separating, which, when you get down to brass tacks, is at the root of both politics and trade. Again, the solution is integration. Efforts to increase it are hugely important in contested territories, and in every nation state where there are minorities.

I keep coming back to the example of British Jews. When the Jews were welcomed into the UK in the twentieth century, they willingly embraced British values and worked hard because they knew that no amount of sympathy or charity would substitute the rewards of self-reliance. When I talk of 'rewards' I don't mean individual riches, but benefits for all of society. In this way, the kindness and compassion shown to the Jewish community by the UK was repaid many times over.

I recently spoke in a debate to commemorate the eightieth anniversary of the *Kindertransport*, which allowed nearly 10,000 Jewish children into the UK from parts of Europe ravaged by antisemitism. An incredible number of these children grew up to be not only scientists, but scientific pioneers; not only lawyers but campaigners for justice; and not only teachers, but role models. Among the children of the *Kindertransport*, there were four future winners of the Nobel Prize. In terms of proportion, that is staggering.

I believe that the Jewish community's outstanding success is in large part explained by their attitude to integration. The three greatest lessons I learned from Jewish people in my early days in the UK were these:

1. Be grateful for the opportunities you've been given.
2. Don't bear grudges or grievances.
3. Never, ever take your freedom for granted.

These precepts are important because they help forge a path to integration.

We should recognise that Jewish people did not integrate after they succeeded; they were successful precisely *because* they integrated.

They didn't see themselves as Jews who happened to live in Britain, but as *British* Jews whose first loyalty was to the country that granted them protection. Members of Britain's Jewish community were, and are, fiercely patriotic.

British Indians, as well as other immigrant groups, can cast themselves in a similar light. Like the Jews in 1930s Europe, the Hindus of 1970s east Africa came to the UK when they were no longer welcome in their own home. Like the Jews, the Hindus in Uganda were singled out as scapegoats for society's ills. And, like the Jewish community, the newly British Hindu community didn't court pity or demand handouts. For us, Britain was the country that gave us freedom, protection and opportunity. It was our community's turn to give back to the country that gave us a chance at a new life. We are all proud of our heritage and religion, and we are bonded to our customs and traditions, but first and foremost we are British, we are lucky to be British and we want to do what's best for our country.

14

AN EAST AFRICAN HOMECOMING

With its coat pegs, corridors and cubbyholes, the Palace of Westminster sometimes feels like a rather grand school. As I go about my political business, I often think back to my days as a pupil at Rock View in Tororo, a much more humble establishment.

For many years, I tried to understand what happened to me there so long ago. Even as a grown adult, I thought about making amends for my chancer-like behaviour when I was a boy. I thought about forgiveness, too, despite being mentally scarred by the beatings I received from my headmaster, Mr Grewal; I knew he had moved from Uganda to England after Amin came to power.

The day before my ennoblement, I hosted a celebration. I had decided to invite Grewal, along with others from my time at school (including my protector Ignatius, now retired after a successful career as a banker in Canada) to a drinks reception. It was a peculiarly special moment for me: a former black sheep was making history standing next to the man who had tortured (and taught) me so many years ago. In a speech, I congratulated Grewal on the fact that one of his former students had become a Lord in the British Parliament.

Tears welled in Grewal's eyes as I spoke. Afterwards, he hugged me and apologised for what he had done. He was proud of me, I suppose. Ignatius witnessed it. It was at that moment that I was finally able to forgive him.

Grewal died in 2015. His widow rang me to see if I could help to get a visa for her son who lived in Dubai to attend the funeral. I immediately rang the British ambassador in Dubai and a visa was arranged. In helping Grewal's family in this way I felt like I'd also somehow settled the hurt that had seethed in me for so many years.

Along with increasing professional political contact with Uganda and Ugandans, these two episodes allowed me to confront my past. Although I obviously felt disillusioned about the regime that had forced my family and I out of the country, I had always maintained a link with Uganda, staying in contact with many friends from there. And now, as I saw through my role as trade envoy to Uganda and Rwanda, a whole new political picture was emerging.

In reality, this shift had started long ago. Uganda had begun to re-engage with positive civic values, international trade and diplomacy, and world matters in general when Yoweri Museveni took power in 1986 following a long bush war. Shortly afterwards, Museveni issued an invitation for Uganda's expelled Asians to come back and help rebuild the country. Many did not take up the offer because they were so well settled in Britain, Canada and other countries. But some did, including my old friends the Madhvani family. Throughout the 1970s, my mentor Manubhai had continued his business activities beyond Uganda, getting involved mainly in glass factories in Lebanon and Saudi Arabia.

On receiving Museveni's invitation, the Madhvanis set about reviving their sugar estate and factory at Kakira near Jinja, with the assistance of the World Bank and the African Development Bank. What courage it must have taken for Manubhai, his brothers and his children, Kamlesh and Shrai, to return to the land where he was imprisoned. It is testament to his character that he was able to find forgiveness in his heart to rekindle his relationship with Uganda.

Today, led by Mayur and Kamlesh (Manubhai's brother and son) as well as the extended family, the Madhvani Group is a behemoth once again. This one enterprise now accounts for more than 10 per cent of Ugandan GDP and employs over 10,000 people. The group has diversified hugely, expanding from sugar production into media, steel, insurance, construction and tourism. The Madhvani's Kakira factory, which I have visited many times, uses the latest turbine technology to generate its own electricity and is also able to put power into Uganda's national energy grid. Beyond Uganda, the Madhvani Group now has an asset base of over $500 million in Africa and the Middle East, with concentrations in agriculture, manufacturing, insurance and tourism.

Other prominent families, such as the Mehtas, also returned to Uganda after Museveni became President. They are once again contributing to both the country's society and economy.

Rather nervously, Sandhya and I first returned to Uganda together in 2012. I was visiting Kampala as part of a delegation of eight British parliamentarians.

The purpose of my visit was to attend an assembly organised by the Inter-Parliamentary Union (IPU) on the theme of 'Parliament and the People: Bridging the Gap'. The IPU is an organisation that brings together the entire world's parliaments, building relationships between lawmakers on issues including defence, human rights and trade.

During this trip, I was privileged to meet senior ministers of the Ugandan government, and His Excellency President Museveni.

At the IPU assembly, I mistakenly sat in one of the seats assigned to Ugandan delegates. The Speaker of the Ugandan Parliament, Rebecca Kadaga, politely asked me to move. I jokingly responded that I was a Ugandan and it was my birth right to sit there, at which point she realised who I was and gave me a hug. This all led to me getting a police motorcade to the President's house for the meeting we had scheduled.

Having read an article I wrote for Uganda's *New Vision* newspaper, which outlined my thoughts on Uganda's transformation under his leadership, Museveni had invited Sandhya and me to have lunch with him at the State House in Kampala. I asked if Mayur Madhvani (Manubhai's brother) might join us, as he knows the President quite well too.

Museveni hugged me on arrival, which was a very unusual way to greet a member of a foreign delegation. Our lunch meeting was meant to last just forty-five minutes, but went on for over two hours! I remember there were so many people waiting to see him, but we just could not stop talking. It was like two long-lost friends meeting after a long time – we instantly clicked.

Museveni was excited that an ex-Ugandan had returned in the form of a British parliamentarian. He then told me how he got involved in guerrilla war against Amin and Obote, which he said was necessary to secure freedom in Uganda, joking that, 'While I was in the bush, you were in Shepherd's Bush!'

He also told me the story of when he went to see his daughter Natasha in Sweden during the war and how she (then four years old) didn't recognise him when she opened the door.

Museveni spoke about his visit to the Swaminarayan Hindu

Temple in Neasden in 1997, where he issued an invitation to Ugandan Asians to return and help rebuild the country. He reminded me, too, that while we Ugandan Asians had been left penniless by our flight from the country, over 250,000 native Ugandans had perished under Idi Amin's dictatorship.

Another thing Museveni mentioned was of his great admiration for David Cameron, paying tribute to him for the diplomatic role he played in reducing conflict in Somalia and his support for the African Union Mission in Somalia.

He also spoke about his vision for Uganda and his aim to increase manufacturing. I remember he mentioned the case for raw coffee and how much more it cost to process, which I said was due to the lack of proper infrastructure.

Museveni referred to several other prominent Ugandan Asian businesspeople that he remembered, some of whom he went to visit in Leicester during a trip in 2008.

The tenor of our conversation shows, I think, that the relationship between Uganda and British Indians of Ugandan heritage is a two-way street and that both sides certainly want the conversation to continue – I myself have had a meeting with Museveni every time I've visited Uganda since.

On that first return visit in 2012, I was amazed at the transformation that has taken place in recent years. The country seemed to be booming, with new businesses everywhere. (The only negative is that this rapid growth has led to heavily congested traffic in Uganda's capital city Kampala.)

While on this first return journey, Sandhya and I briefly visited Tororo, but there was not time to really go back to my childhood haunts. That would have to wait for another trip.

Since gaining independence in 1962, Uganda has certainly been on a political rollercoaster ride: a socialist government under Obote, a brutal dictator in Idi Amin, a long civil war and now, finally, a more democratic ethos under the leadership of Museveni, which is characterised by a strong resolve to forge international trade links.

There is still work to do. The matter of a democratic transfer of power to a younger generation of leaders is not proving easy to solve. Involvement in two wars in neighbouring Congo between 1998 and 2002 has had domestic ramifications, economically and politically. Corruption is still a problem among some sectors of the elite; this culture then filters down into ordinary life, especially if public servants are not paid properly or on time.

However, Museveni deserves great praise for the way he has encouraged inward investment, and for how he has used private sector growth to power the Ugandan economy. He has also been one of the few political leaders to focus on improving security in the east African region. To have come through such a challenging history and now boast annual growth figures of an average of 5 per cent – a figure that would be the envy of most countries in the world – is a very fine achievement in itself, and Uganda still has so much potential for future growth.

Real progress has been made in the area of energy, and Britain has played a role in that. Total trade in goods and services (i.e. exports plus imports) between the UK and Uganda in 2016 saw a 59.5 per cent increase compared to only the previous year. This is mainly due to the increasing trade in services and the discovery of approximately 6.5 billion barrels of oil in Uganda. British policy reflects the growing importance it attaches to trade with Uganda. UK Export Finance – the government's export credit agency – has expanded its total risk appetite to over £600 million in Uganda. This includes £215 million for a British company to build a new airport in the Kabaale region – the largest-ever loan UK Export Finance has made to an African government – as well as supporting a number of large projects (ranging from construction and engineering to banking and financial services) totalling over £2 billion, such as the building of a refinery and oil pipeline. Britain is also Uganda's second largest provider of development assistance, giving around £100 million every year to alleviate poverty and boost economic growth.

It's a good investment for Britain. Elevated by its recent oil finds, Uganda is now a leading light in east Africa, with a vibrant economy, a young and well-educated workforce and a business environment primed for international investment.

There are still some weak spots, however. According to the Ugandan Ministry of Tourism, the number of tourists visiting Uganda in 2011 had fallen to 76,000 from the previous year's 149,000. Uganda is the kind of place lots of people should want to visit – it has many natural advantages as a tourist destination. Unlocking the great potential in the country's tourism market will allow Uganda's economy to reach even greater heights. Partly the blockage is to do with increasing security, but the country also suffers from negative perceptions based on recent history. In addition, the treatment of LGBT people in Uganda has had an effect on how the country is viewed internationally.

Politically, however, Uganda has displayed admirable leadership. It has been at the forefront of finding a solution to the problems in Somalia through its leadership of the African Union Mission. I know that when President Museveni visited London in May 2013,

David Cameron thanked Uganda for supporting Somalia's (still uneasy) transition to a federal government.

On my appointment as trade envoy in 2016, I found myself at the heart of the operation that drives the wide-ranging and close relationship between Uganda and the UK, in areas such as security, politics, development, education and commercial activity, with a particular focus on gas, energy and oil. But I had already been involved informally in forging some of these links. In 2014, the then Lord Mayor of the City of London, Alderman Fiona Woolf, made her first visit to Uganda, taking with her a delegation of UK companies from financial and legal services, and the energy sector. This trip underlined the priority the UK places on the present importance of the Ugandan market and the significance of its future potential.

In addition, also in 2014, representatives from twenty energy companies participated in the Aberdeen and Grampian Chamber of Commerce and London Chamber of Commerce's annual trade mission to Uganda. These two Chambers (Aberdeen being Britain's oil capital and London being the financial capital) are regular visitors to the region.

The mission was led by my good friend and fellow Ugandan Asian Subhash Thakrar, the past chairman of the London Chamber of Commerce, and Julien Masse, of the Aberdeen Chamber. Its participants had a range of objectives, including looking for local representatives, distributors, agents and clients, with some companies researching the Ugandan market for the first time and others building on existing contacts.

As trade envoy, I work closely with the Department for International Development (DFID) to support Uganda's development and economic growth. In an average year, the DFID provides more than £90 million to support Uganda's efforts in critical areas such as health and family planning, private sector development and tackling corruption. Between 2011 and 2015, the UK will have enabled more than 400,000 people to access family planning, distributed 5 million bed nets to prevent malaria and helped 300,000 people to cope with the effects of climate change in Karamoja – the poorest area of Uganda.

One of the programmes supported by the DFID is Trademark East Africa, which is boosting growth and job opportunities by cutting the cost and time it takes to move goods in and out of Customs, and building vital infrastructure across east Africa. The key achievements of this programme will include: constructing a 'one-stop' border post between Uganda and South Sudan to cut time wasted in Customs; cutting the time it takes to move a container across Uganda by twenty-one hours (a reduction of 40 per cent); and cutting general waiting times at Ugandan Customs by a day and a half.

All these initiatives are designed to increase regional competitiveness by reducing transit time along the transport corridors of the east African Community (Uganda, Burundi, Kenya, Rwanda, South Sudan and Tanzania). Anyone who has seen the queues of trucks at African border posts (often up to twenty miles long) will know how important this is.

I find the trade envoyship fascinating. In any given day, I might be working with the British High Commission in Kampala to boost the UK's reputation as a business partner, utilising connections with the Ugandan government to improve our business links or assisting individual UK firms of differing sizes on specific issues relating to market access.

This last part is key, especially with respect to smaller firms. Whatever government programmes are put in place, the lifeblood of any economy is small businesses. It has been really exciting for me to bring together my interest in SMEs with my export brief.

I know from speaking to the country's ministers that Uganda places great importance on supporting its SMEs, which are the cornerstone of industrial development, accounting for some 90 per cent of Uganda's private sector and providing some 50 to 60 per cent of the country's total employment.

Another part of my role involves making sure Ugandan politicians, civil servants and businesspeople feel welcome in Britain. This is made easier by the fact that there are now so many people with Ugandan roots in the UK Parliament: Shailesh Vara and Priti Patel in the House of Commons and, in the House of Lords, the Archbishop of York, John Sentamu, Baroness Shriti Vadera, Lord Mohammed Sheikh (president of the Conservative Muslim Forum), Lord Verjee, myself and the recently appointed Lord Jitesh Gadhia.

Yoweri Museveni's high-profile visit to the UK in May 2014, which I helped to organise, was a great success. The delegation included seven Ugandan ministers and approximately forty senior officials. During his trip, Museveni held talks with British civil servants and prospective investors about the security situation in the region, focusing on South Sudan.

Museveni also addressed the UK–Uganda Business Forum on Uganda's investment potential. This event was attended by over 100 key UK businesses, including Tullow Oil and Standard Chartered.

A surprise call came from Museveni some time later. He was planning to be in the UK for a conference, and wanted an opportunity to speak to British companies who were considering doing business in Uganda. Naturally, I obliged. Despite the very short notice (two weeks!), I managed to organise an event in the House of Lords with a selection of some of the best of British businesses.

During his address, Museveni hinted at his disappointment that the UK was not as engaged in Uganda as it could or should be. When a member of the audience asked about China, which is a dominant commercial player in Uganda, Museveni's response was telling. He said, 'I do not speak Chinese. I speak English. But the Chinese are the ones who offered to build our infrastructure at a time when Britain turned its back. What choice did we have?' Taken at face value, this statement appears to criticise Britain, but the implicit (and more positive) message was clear: Britain has a natural advantage in Uganda because of our shared history. Why are we not focusing on supporting a shared prosperity? I saw this as Museveni reaching out. I hope that British companies will reach out in return.

In terms of investment, Britain, with over £2 billion in Uganda, remains the country's largest cumulative investor. But we need to keep on our toes – China, Germany and many other countries are constantly trying to steal our lunch!

Sometimes our efforts at selling Britain in Uganda seem to stall. Things start well: proposals are well received; everyone seems to be on the same page; memoranda of understanding are enthusiastically submitted to the relevant departments by British firms. And then… nothing. No feedback, no progress. There needs to be more transparency and accountability in government departments in Uganda (and in other African countries), as otherwise it reflects poorly on a great country.

At the same time, British firms themselves need to be more proactive. They need to look to expand the opportunities that those already operating in Uganda are demonstrating can be the basis of significant success.

All this is why I am these days almost constantly on a plane to Uganda, trying to drum up business for Britain and, just as importantly, to help make that business happen. I also perform a similar role in Rwanda, which is right next door to Uganda and intimately connected to it, but which in business terms is characterised by different investment opportunities and challenges.

Since the genocide in 1994, Rwanda has transformed into one of the most impressive countries in Africa, achieving prolonged economic growth despite a lack of natural resources. It is probably the safest country in Africa and corruption of any sort is not tolerated. In terms of women in Parliament and leadership roles generally, it is in the first rank globally.

Britain has played a supportive role in Rwanda's transformation, and this has provided a number of opportunities for British firms in terms of infrastructure and the agricultural sector. We are helping to build on a good base. Rwanda is ranked twenty-nine among 190 economies for ease of doing business (according to the latest World Bank ratings) and its capital, Kigali, is considered the greenest city in Africa, environmentally speaking. With RwandAir's flight from Kigali to Gatwick now fully operational, these opportunities for Britain to be involved in an African success story will only grow.

The British government has specifically supported the government of Paul Kagame, who was re-elected for a third term in 2017. Yet Kagame's victory in Rwanda was not welcomed everywhere. Several British publications and international organisations were critical of his leadership style, or focused on the difficulties faced by the opposition.

It's important to see these things in context. I've seen countless attempts at democracy fail in Africa while the West looked the other way. Africa's history of dictatorships, tribalism and instability is a great strain on the continent, but the trend towards democracy is clearly going in the right direction.

Democracies such as Rwanda's are young. They do not have the benefit of centuries of constitutional precedent, nor the luxury of revered institutions that can adapt to changing circumstances, as we do in Britain. We should support any country in Africa that is trying to make democracy work, despite imperfections.

It's not only Britons that can so often lose their perspective when it comes to fledgling democracies. This seems to be a habit of many Western countries. We choose to lecture rather than to guide; to grandstand rather than to coax. It is perhaps little wonder that as Western (in particular British) commercial interests in Africa decline, the Chinese and their 'no questions asked' approach gains more traction. We in the West should seek a middle ground.

Democracies always need work, wherever they are. In Britain, for example, we have only fairly recently devolved powers to regions and local communities, and enlisted more elected mayors and police commissioners. The development of wider access to political power is an ongoing process here, as well as in Africa.

In some respects, despite the two countries' differences, Uganda provides a model for Rwanda. In Uganda, too, there have been real strides towards freedom, irrespective of problems with leadership succession. When I visit Uganda now, I myself feel much freer and safer than I did when I was there as a young man.

I will describe one of these visits to Uganda in more detail, as it coincided with some big news for me. Before doing so, however,

I want to reflect on my main achievements so far as trade envoy, which include: reintroducing direct flights from the UK to Rwanda with RwandAir; overseeing the construction of Kabaale International Airport in Uganda's western region (UK companies are involved in this project, which is near the Kaiso–Tonya oil fields and the Uganda Oil Refinery); the doubling of UK Export Finance demonstrating Britain's confidence in doing business in the country; and promoting the UK's strengths in project delivery and technology, and the quality of our oil and gas projects. This includes the purchase of two A330-800 airliners which will fly direct between London and Entebbe from 2020.

It is tremendously exciting to have helped drive all this progress, but it still does not seem like nearly enough. It is only the beginning, in fact. I am confident that we will easily increase our bilateral trade between the UK and Uganda by five-fold from the current £188 million (as the figures stood in 2017). In fact, I believe that we can go even further by increasing trade with Uganda to over £2 billion over the next few years.

15

BACK TO THE ROCK

In June 2016, I invited my beloved elder brother Manoj and old friend Ignatius to join me on a trip to Uganda. It was the first time either of them had been back. Convening at Schiphol Airport in Amsterdam because they were both coming from Canada, we boarded a mid-morning flight to Entebbe. I spent the time reminiscing with Ignatius about our journey in the opposite direction, forty-five years previously. So much had happened to both of us, and to Manoj, too, but here we were again, joshing away as if we were still teenagers.

On arrival in Entebbe, I felt the familiar kick of excitement about being in Africa again. I was whisked off to the residence of the then British High Commissioner, Alison Blackburne, where I was spending the night as a guest.

The house is at 33 Kyadondo Road, Nakasero. Rented from the Mehta family, this property was one of the locations used in the film *The Last King of Scotland* (based on the novel of the same name about Idi Amin and his doctor, written by my friend Giles Foden). In the film, it played the role of State House. Although now a thriving Kampala suburb, Nakasero was a place redolent of dark history. The State Research Bureau, the intelligence agency established by

Amin after his coup, had its headquarters there, which over the next few years became a scene of torture and executions.

Alison was an extremely gracious host and, as per the norm on these visits, gave me a political and economic briefing over breakfast the next day. Then I set out on my official duties, which included appointments with the Kampala Capital City Authority and the Uganda National Roads Authority. I had lunch with the Minister of Energy and Mineral Development, Irene Muloni, and then met with Minister of Foreign Affairs, Sam Kutesa. The rest of the afternoon was spent in close conclave with President Museveni – I knew him pretty well by now.

The next couple of days were pretty hectic, comprising meetings with the Ministry of Trade at the Serena Hotel and the Ministry of Works and Transport, with Tullow Uganda and the Department of International Development, and with the Rural Electrification Agency. Finally, on the night of the third day, I could let my hair down a bit at a cocktail party at the British High Commission, which was attended by over 150 business people at which I gave a speech on new UK–Uganda relations.

Later that night, I caught up with Manoj and Ignatius. They informed me they had got a bit lost on leaving Entebbe Airport, going to the Speke Hotel in the centre of the city instead of the Speke Resort at Munyonyo on the edge of Lake Victoria. This experience, at more or less midnight in downtown Kampala, ended up with them being hauled over by the police for driving down a one-way street!

'This is usually the kind of thing that happens to you, Dolar,' quipped Ignatius.

'Not any more,' I said.

'Not now he is a Lord,' said my brother.

And so it would go on, over the next few days, them teasing me as we began a journey that would take us right back to our roots as young lads, trying to make our way in (and out of) Amin's Uganda.

The next morning we set off for Tororo in a vehicle loaned to us by an old friend, who was now established in business in Uganda. On the way we crossed the Nile and the equator – always an emotional staging post for anyone living in eastern Uganda. It made me think of all the times I had done the same journey with my parents and siblings.

On the way, we bought maize from street traders. Roasted at the roadside, sprinkled with salt, chilli and lime, this really brought the memories flooding back. Known as *mahindi*, probably because it was called 'Indian corn' in colonial days, these are cobs of starchy, hard field corn, mature but light green, almost white in colour. It's not at all like the sweet, soft-yellow corn that is common in other parts of the world. Sweetcorn would scorch in the charcoal braziers that this delicacy is cooked over before being thrust in car windows. I have always thought of these hard, chewy cobs as the true taste of east Africa. If I were a poet I would choose them as the symbol of east African toughness – that same toughness we east African Asians carried across to Britain and other countries.

Talking of toughness, our base in Tororo was the house of Sanjay Tanna. As solid as a wildebeest and as cunning as mongoose, he is a good friend and, really, just an extraordinary character. One of the few Indians who managed to stay in the country all through Amin's time and after, Sanjay is an amazingly resourceful man. Along with his family, he has made and, through the ups and downs of regime change, lost several fortunes.

One good story Sanjay told us over lunch that day was how he was once penniless, having had all the stock of his shop stolen by soldiers during the civil war. Thinking it was all over, he happened to meet an old Gujarati wholesaler whom his father had once done a kindness, two decades earlier. The old man resupplied him on the basis of trust. Once again, Sanjay was able to rebuild his fortunes. The story is, I think, typical of both the resilience of the individual east African Indian but also helps demonstrate how the whole network continues to support itself, both in east Africa and beyond.

When I think of the word 'resilience', I think of Sanjay, not least because he took the big step of becoming an MP in Uganda, the first Indian to do so since Jayantbhai Madhvani and Mahendrabhai Mehta back in the 1960s. Although out of office as I write, Sanjay is still pretty much a local hero among the people of Tororo, speaking up for them when vested interests threaten their wellbeing and prosperity. His own business is based on being the agent for a number of Western and South African companies in eastern Uganda, but he has never let that get in the way of being a voice for ordinary Ugandans.

Sanjay mingles with the people of Tororo freely, helping them as if they were his own relatives. He engages them on local issues, mixing Luganda, English and Kiswahili in fluent, jokey conversation. But behind the jokes is a real respect for indigenous Ugandans. They just love him. So does Museveni, who has often lent Sanjay his support, even though he is an independent politician standing against Museveni's own party. Sanjay himself is a supporter of Museveni personally but quite critical of his party, the National Resistance Movement. He is fond of asking, quite loudly, how much of their programme have they achieved?

Good question; complicated answers.

Sanjay's fearlessness has, however, made him some enemies in Uganda. I must say it was a bit of shock to discover that he drives around with an automatic pistol in his glove compartment, as well as being accompanied by an armed security guard.

Conveyed in this fashion in Sanjay's 4x4, we drove after lunch to my old secondary school at Manjasi. I had arranged sixty computers to be bought for it and was keen to see whether they were in use. They had been installed, I found, but the software was not quite up and running. There was a lot of work to be done, in fact, in getting Manjasi back to its former high standard. I resolved to make further charitable donations.

It breaks my heart to see Africa go backwards. I am afraid, despite the best efforts of the staff, that this is what has happened at Manjasi. But it is a common phenomenon in Africa. One must go on in hope, trusting that people will build for themselves as well as relying on charity.

I laid a wreath at the grave of a former headmaster at Manjasi, Mr Townsend, who (unlike Grewal at my primary school) had been an inspirational figure for me. He had been working with unpromising material; it was not his fault that I failed all my exams, it was mine.

Afterwards, Manoj, Ignatius and myself gave talks in the school assembly. We tried to explain to the students how we, too, had sat in these same buildings, how we, too, had had the dreams of youngsters. I told the pupils that if they extended their horizons, worked hard and stayed hopeful, there was nothing to stop them achieving success in whatever field they chose. They just needed to open their eyes to what was possible. They needed to look beyond Manjasi,

beyond Tororo, beyond Uganda, even – but never forget where
they had come from.

'Hey, Dolar!' Ignatius called from over by the fence, once we had
emerged from assembly. 'Do you remember when we use to crawl
through here to go see the girls?'

I grinned. There had been happy times here, too, despite my
constant failures as a student. We revisited the good times for half
an hour or so by making the trip to the girls' school next door,
which my sisters had attended, as had Ignatius's sister Ninette.

Later, we went to Rock View School. I stood on the dusty spot
where Grewal had beaten me in public. Despite the hot sunlight of
the Ugandan afternoon, I believe I shivered a bit. So much time
had passed; was I still to be plagued by these bad memories? Was I
any different now than the shamed boy of the past? I felt unsteady,
like I didn't know who I was. Then I heard, from high above me,
the call of a buzzard.

Looking up, I saw the shape of a large brown bird circling Tororo
Rock, the visual focus of so many of my teenage glooms and hopes.
Then I knew somehow that it was all right, this accommodation
between past and present, and between Uganda and Britain, which
has conditioned the narrative of my life. It was as if the buzzard was
lifting all my feelings as it rose on its thermal, high above the school
and my old life. I was able to see the past, including my visions of
the future when I was young, in the same wide view afforded the
buzzard by its circling, ever ascending height.

After leaving Rock View, we visited the waterworks where Ignatius's father was manager, and then went into central Tororo, where
my father's shop had been and where I had lived as a teenager.

By this stage, the weather had turned. It was pouring with rain:

a real, old-style tropical downpour such as I remembered from the old days. In the midst of this heavy rain, as we drove, Ignatius spoke. I can't remember what he said and may not even have heard, so loud was the tattoo of rain on the roof of the car. But what I saw was his young face – the face of the past, seen in aspect beside me now and beside me then, mooching teenagers as we were, here in Tororo. Leaning on a pillar in his leather jacket, as I recall, the young Ignatius was gazing in rapture at the face of a pretty young girl in a passing vehicle, just arrived in town.

It was the face of Roma, the woman who would become his wife. And I seem to remember him saying to me then or shortly afterwards that he would marry that girl. Young men say this kind of thing, of course, but in this instance it happened to come true. I thought, as we drove along through the downpour, of my own wife Sandhya and all the love and support she has given me in my life. I have been lucky in that, as in so many things.

The rain continued to fall. When I visited our old shop, now a half-functional hotel adjacent to the main roundabout in Tororo, I was moved to tears. It was odd to look at the damaged plasterwork in the pillars of the building; I felt as if part of my own psychic fabric was bound up with that damage. But it also struck me that life was still going on, in and around this building, people and vehicles splashing past, looking quizzically at this group of *wahindis* (as Ugandans call us) who were curiously inspecting the old structure that must have been through many hands during all the years of war and misfortune.

'I have seen enough wars, bloodshed and fighting to last me a lifetime,' announced Sanjay that evening, as the four of us sat on his veranda enjoying a barbeque. He had this ingenious little African charcoal stove, and was flash-frying fish on a steel plate on top.

'Whenever I see any disturbance in Uganda today, and it still happens, I try to remind people that we are all brothers and sisters. It doesn't matter what race or tribe you are from.' He threw a handful of spices on the sizzling fish.

'You seem to be as accepted as a Ugandan', Manoj commented, 'in a way we never were when we were here.'

'I am Ugandan,' said Sanjay. 'It's as simple as that. But it's about "being Ugandan" not being a fixed idea. My father always told me that when the ideas that are out there are all used up, several times over, they need to be replenished. You have to allow something new to develop from within … and that is what has happened in Uganda, just as it should be happening within all of us, all the time.'

As I was listening to this conversation, thinking about how it applied to me and my own history, a text pinged into my mobile. It was Mark, my chief of staff, telling me that David Cameron had resigned, bringing a sudden end to his six-year premiership after the British electorate took the momentous decision to ignore his entreaties to stay in the European Union. I myself was one of those who supported Remain *because* of Cameron.

I stumbled off into the garden in shock. Breaking a self-denying decree and endless promises to Sandhya and my doctor, I lit a cigarette. I looked up into the big African sky, feeling that part of my world had fallen in, crashing down in the gap between one cloud and the next. So much of my life, my time, my whole being over the past decade had been associated with David Cameron. Together, with Andrew Feldman (then Conservative Party chairman) and others, we had brought the British Indian population back to its natural home among Tories.

And now it was all over, or so it seemed. Like so many others before him, Cameron had fallen victim to events – the great enemy of the politician but also the source of political opportunity. Looking at the flame trees in Sanjay's garden – in the home of this man who had suffered far greater turbulence than I ever had – I felt a sudden, anxious urge to be back in Westminster and at the heart of the events that had toppled Cameron. But I wasn't there. I couldn't be there. I was in Uganda, the land of my birth.

There was a divine irony at play, surely, working across time and place. Uganda, the site of so much historical instability, sends me to London; now it was calm in Uganda, and London was in chaos. I thought of the presentation within Hinduism of Krishna as time, the destroyer of worlds, and almost at the same moment of some lines in the *Bhavagad Gita* that suggest both permanence and transience in the same everlasting instant: 'There was never a time when I was not, or when you or these kings were not present. Nor is it a fact that hereafter we shall all cease to be.' The context is reincarnation, but whether you believe in that or not these are powerful lines, speaking to a feeling we all have, I think, that everything that comes to pass has been stored up in the past, and that our being somehow survives the apparent destruction of time.

At first, however, I couldn't see what good could come of Cameron's resignation. I still think we are feeling the effects of it, both in the Conservative Party and as a nation (not that he had much choice, once the British people had made their decision on Brexit, however marginal that decision was).

As I stood in Sanjay's garden, I resolved over the next few days to try to put the resignation out of my head until I got home, but the whole of that night as I lay in bed, I couldn't help thinking about the political and personal ramifications of what had happened.

The next day, the political news from Britain was sharply put in perspective by a visit to the hospital in Busolwe, the village in which I was born that has now grown into a town. When I was living in Busolwe, there was no hospital. In fact, my own mother was a midwife who had helped in the births of many children, both Asian and African, as a direct result of the community's lack of medical facilities.

So, I was quite interested to see what had been achieved since our family had lived in Busolwe, and took a tour of the place, along with Manoj, Ignatius and Sanjay. Built in 1969 for a capacity of 500 beds, the hospital's stated current capacity is for between 100 and 250 patients, though there were far fewer than that there on the day I visited. It serves a regional population of over 250,000, as well as many others from neighbouring districts. There are four wards: male, female, maternity and children's, together with a range of outpatient services, including antenatal and postnatal care. There are also specialised diabetic, tuberculosis and hypertension clinics.

All that may sound good on paper, but Busolwe hospital was in pretty bad shape the day we visited. It was generally run down, with both the main hospital and staff quarters looking dilapidated. Patients could be better described as surviving rather than being comfortable. Many had no linen on their beds, for example, and did the best they could in concrete-lined wards, with food and night soil pots lying around. There was inadequate space in the current children's ward; the X-ray and ultrasound machines did not work; there was no ambulance or administration vehicle for staff; there was no incinerator to dispose of used products; and there was no accommodation on site for the relatives of inpatients to stay in.

All this is fairly normal for a hospital in a poor part of rural

Africa, but I felt I needed to do something. Speaking to the staff en masse, I immediately pledged funds to build a new maternity ward at Busolwe Hospital.

What I had seen in terms of the low levels of even primary care shocked me, although I knew it was the norm. When I got home from Uganda, I would begin a series of communications that would lead to the twinning of Busolwe Hospital and Leicester Royal Infirmary. Leicester seemed the right choice of location in Britain to me, as the city was where so many expelled Ugandan Asians ended up. The planned twinning of the two hospitals will likely involve visits by medical practitioners based at Leicester to Busolwe, either in a voluntary capacity or as part of electives and training rotations.

I am hopeful that this process, along with further fundraising efforts among the Uganda Asian diaspora, will help the development of the hospital at Busolwe, but these things take time and continued effort.

Once the visit was over, my companions and I went to see what had happened to the house in Busolwe in which I was born, and the adjacent shop. An African family was living there now. Although a little surprised, the lady of the house greeted us with customary Ugandan politeness and showed us round. The door of the room in which I used to sleep was kept shut. The person inside was ill, we were told. Strangely, the storeroom at the back, or what had been the storeroom in my childhood, had been turned into a little cinema. I thought of my own entrepreneurial efforts at showing films when I was a teenager – I don't think my father would have allowed me to show films at home!

I had a powerful memory of walking on this floor (was it the exact same one?) in bare feet. Weirdly, this sense of memory arose not in my brain but began in the soles of my feet themselves and then up through my body, as if it were sediment becoming swirled up in a jar of liquid.

It was very dark in the house. As is always said to happen on such occasions, the place seemed much smaller than I remembered. As I walked about, I had a flash vision of my parents sitting at the rough-hewn kitchen table under the light of a hissing paraffin lamp, of my sisters moving to and fro in their rustling saris, of the Manoj of the past, pedalling away at his sewing machine – the same Manoj who now stood beside me in his bright Canadian casuals, the same but different, changed as we all were by time, even though he was nattering on like he used to do. A vision then of my family as it was, when we were not much wealthier than the family who lived in the house now – but happy enough, happy enough.

I felt a little unsteady as we ducked under the doorway and came back out into the light. What was all this noise? A crowd had gathered outside. Somehow, journalists had discovered about the return of 'Lord Popat' to his native turf and I had to give a couple of interviews. As I was speaking, my mind kept turning again to Parliament and Conservative Party headquarters, and all the interviews, discussions and arguments that must be going on there in the wake of Cameron's resignation.

Questions of my own filled my mind as I answered those of the Ugandan journalists about my trip. What was I going to do? Was there really a place for me in the Tory administration, now that Cameron was gone? Who would replace him? Would they do a good job? We know the answers to some of these questions now, but this was the pattern of my thoughts on that day, which perversely was as filled with sun as the previous day had been filled with rain.

During the afternoon, deciding that I needed to relax my mind as much as my body, I went for a round of golf on the course at Tororo under the Rock, walking that same fairway along the edges I had so often wandered as an excluded boy, watching colonial officials or their latter-day British equivalents play. But now here I was with my own trolley and card – official, legit, green fees paid, accepted. I played a fairly good round, accompanied by the writer Giles Foden (who was in the country at the same time), and the club professional, whom I was delighted to find to be of Ugandan Asian stock.

Reaching the final tee, I set up, ready to swing, but then paused as my mind filled with one of those mantras that are swapped between golfers with as much sense of their value as rupees and thalers were passed between old-time Gujarati traders. The words of the great Ben Hogan, generally considered one of the best players in the history of the game, swelled in my consciousness: 'The most important shot in golf is the next one.'

This is true – in golf, politics, business and life in general, whether you are an immigrant or not. We just have to see how things go. But I'm ready, just as I always was – and at least I've got shoes now!

I believe that back in the days when I didn't have shoes – and for quite a long time afterwards – people underestimated me. I probably underestimated myself, as well. And, despite the enormous strides the continent has made in the past twenty-five years, people still make the mistake of underestimating Africa. It can have a bright future, but we need to develop the next generation of businesspeople and politicians, and ensure that the best principles of trade and democracy are embedded across the continent. This is a worthy aim, and one to which I would happily devote the rest of my life.

AFTERWORD BY MORARI BAPU

Before I started putting this book together, I discussed it with my guru, Morari Bapu, who – as always – filled me with confidence and ideas. I can never truly explain how much his teachings have inspired me to be a better human being, and I was truly humbled when he offered to provide a concluding message for the book. I have referred to Bapu as being like secondary school when it came to my experiences with Hinduism, so for me, this message is like graduating from university with honours. Here is the translation of the final word, from a man who inspires millions of ordinary people like me around the world to try to be a little bit better every single day.

* * *

My close friend Lord Dolarbhai Popat,

His position as a Lord who occupies a place of honour in the House of Lords in Great Britain gives us all a sense of proudness. However, above all, he is a man that possesses human qualities such as humbleness, simplicity and a natural instinct to keep his feet firmly planted on mother earth. These qualities make him a centre of attraction for all who happen to meet him.

I have known him closely and inside out now for many years. He is a patriarch of his family and a humble servant of the community, ever ready to work for the benefit of those in need. He rarely says no to anyone who approaches him for help and guidance.

As a Lord, he undertakes his duties in Parliament with grace and dignity; this is something I am personally very proud of.

> para hita sarisa dharma nahiṃ bhāī
> para pīḍaā sama nahiṃ adhamāī
> RAMCHARITMANAS, UTARKAAND [7-40-1]

In the above couplet (*chopai*), Tulsidasji declared that the highest spiritual virtue is benevolence, and no sin as vile as oppressing others.

I see this *chopai* in Dolarbhai's character.

He has an extremely happy family life and an outstanding feature of his personality is that he is ever ready to serve others physically, mentally and materially.

He is associated with several countries and cultures and he undertakes his work with a dignity that befits his position. I have also seen on my travels with him how he is his natural self in villages, farms and huts of the poor. These qualities are, in my opinion, very rarely found and nourished.

People are often surprised and even stunned by the devotion that he and his entire family bears towards me and my Ram Katha. The personality of Dolarbhai flowers and flows in all the three streams of life, political, social and cultural, and it gives me immense happiness to watch these three streams mixing and intermingling in him.

I eternally pray to Hanumanji that the almighty may grant Dolarbhai plenty of opportunities for growth and pleasant experiences and may he stay happy for ever and ever.

Stay happy, Dolarbhai!

With remembrances of Ram,

Bapu
Chitrakutdham, Talgajarda
3 May 2019

ACKNOWLEDGEMENTS

When Michael Dobbs first suggested I should write my story, I was dumbfounded! Thank you, Michael, for planting that seed many years ago, and to Olivia Beattie and her team at Biteback for helping it to blossom.

I am indebted to Giles Foden for his extraordinary ability to bring all of these stories and events together. From huddling over coffee in the House of Lords to wandering around the landscapes of Uganda, Giles was always excellent company and never shied away from the difficult questions. Giles – thank you for all of your patience and perseverance.

My wonderful wife Sandhya went back through fifty-odd years of photos (many of which I'd rather not have seen again!) to give these stories even more colour.

Ameet Jogia and Mark Fletcher have probably done more for this book than anybody else. They've read every version, corrected many errors and managed to make this book a reality. It's a strange feeling that these two young men seem to know me better than I know myself sometimes, and they're the best team I could have ever asked for. Thanks, guys. Now, what's next?